Sitka

By Penny Rennick and L.J. Campbell

Published by
The Alaska Geographic Society
Anchorage, Alaska

COVER: *Mount Edgecumbe dominates views from Sitka's waterfront. (Harry M. Walker)*

TITLE PAGE: *St. Michael's Cathedral recalls Sitka's Russian heritage. (Scott Chambers)*

LIBRARY OF CONGRESS CATALOGING-IN-PUBLICATION DATA

Rennick, Penny.
    Sitka / by Penny Rennick and L.J. Campbell.
       p.   cm. -- (Alaska geographic guides)
    Includes bibliographical references (p.   ) and index.
    ISBN 1-56661-029-X (pbk.)
    1. Sitka (Alaska)--Guidebooks. 2. Sitka (Alaska)--Description and travel. 3. Sitka Region (Alaska)--Guidebooks. 4. Sitka Region (Alaska)--Description and travel. I. Campbell, L.J. (Linda Johnson), 1957- . II. Title. III. Series.
F914.S6R46 1995
979.8'2--dc20

           95-40004
           CIP

COLOR SEPARATIONS BY: Graphic Chromatics
PRINTED BY: The Hart Press

MAPS AND DESIGN BY: Kathy Doogan

The Alaska Geographic Society
P.O. Box 93370 • Anchorage, AK 99509

PRINTED IN U.S.A.

Contents

Totems like Gaanaxadi/ Raven Crest pole commemorate Tlingit culture. (Ernest Manewal)

Acknowledgements

ALASKA GEOGRAPHIC® readers have written us on many occasions asking for detailed information on visiting communities and attractions in Alaska. To answer these questions and to encourage others to experience some of the best that Alaska has to offer, The Alaska Geographic Society is producing a new series of guides, in addition to our regular quarterly monographs. To launch *ALASKA GEOGRAPHIC*® *GUIDES*, we chose Sitka, a major community in Southeast Alaska that at one time outclassed San Francisco in both commerce and elegance. The former capital of Russian America and Alaska's first capital under the U.S. flag, Sitka looks to tourism, fishing and services to sustain its vitality amid a classically beautiful setting on Baranof Island.

Penny Rennick, editor of *ALASKA GEOGRAPHIC*®, and L.J. Campbell, staff writer, prepared the text, with the exception of the Sitka chronology for which we thank Joan M. Antonson, Alaska state historian. We also thank geologist Jim Riehle, with the U.S. Geological Survey, for sharing his expertise about Mount Edgecumbe volcano. We acknowledge the help of many residents of Sitka who provided information and encouragement for the book, in particular, Cyndy Rogers, program director of the Alaska Raptor Rehabilitation Center, Don Muller of Old Harbor Books and Mary Stensvold of the U.S. Forest Service for reviewing the entire manuscript. We thank Gary Gauthier, superintendent, and Sue Thorsen, museum specialist, for providing information and reviewing sections relating to Sitka National Historical Park, and Leslie Slater of the U.S. Fish and Wildlife Service's Alaska Maritime National Wildlife Refuge for reviewing the St. Lazaria text. We also thank Doug Stockdale, with the U.S. Forest Service in Sitka, and Rollo Pool for their help in reviewing sections of the text and providing information. Peter Corey, director, and Lisa Bykonen shared information on Sheldon Jackson Museum and College. Anne Shepard, director of visitor services for the Sitka Convention and Visitors Bureau, and her staff, provided overall guidance to the many visitor attractions at Sitka.

A City of Consequence

Sitka is a cozy, yet cosmopolitan city wrapped in spectacular scenery. Its union of ocean, forests and mountains tempts photographers at every turn.

It is a place rich in Russian history and Native culture. Thousands of people come ashore here each summer to take in Sitka's heritage and admire its nature, making it one of Southeast's most visited ports.

Sitka is accustomed to visitors. During Russian rule in the 1800s, it was the largest city on the continent's west coast, an affluent center of commerce known as "Paris of the Pacific."

Today the waterfront is even busier. Most people come and go from Sitka by boat. Cruise ships arrive almost daily in summer, occasionally as many as four anchoring in Sitka Sound at a time. Charter boats, tour operators, bus drivers, museum staffs and shop owners set their hours accordingly. The state ferries deliver travelers from afar as well, along with villagers from more remote Southeast locations who come to Sitka for shopping and dinner.

Sitka also is the gathering place each summer for senior citizens taking part in Elderhostel programs, to study Alaska history, art and other topics. And each June, the city hosts its acclaimed Sitka Summer Music Festival and Island Institute humanities conference, attracting internationally known musicians and writers to perform and teach. Sitkans immerse themselves in the cultural

There are varying interpretations of the meaning for the word "Sitka," but the most common seems to be "by the sea" or "on the outside," referring to Sitka's position on the Pacific or outside coast of Baranof Island.

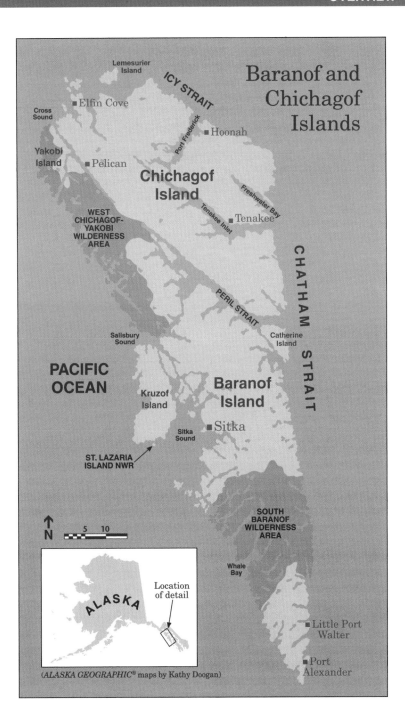

Baranof and Chichagof Islands

Lemesurier Island

ICY STRAIT

Elfin Cove

Cross Sound

Port Frederick

Hoonah

Yakobi Island

Pelican

Chichagof Island

Freshwater Bay

WEST CHICHAGOF-YAKOBI WILDERNESS AREA

Tenakee Inlet

Tenakee

CHATHAM STRAIT

PERIL STRAIT

Salisbury Sound

Catherine Island

PACIFIC OCEAN

Kruzof Island

Baranof Island

Sitka

Sitka Sound

ST. LAZARIA ISLAND NWR

SOUTH BARANOF WILDERNESS AREA

N
5   10

Whale Bay

ALASKA

Location of detail

Little Port Walter

Port Alexander

(*ALASKA GEOGRAPHIC*® maps by Kathy Doogan)

About 9,000 people live in Sitka, on the outer coast of Baranof Island. (Ernest Manewal)

crossroads that is their town.

In the peak of all this, particularly when several thousand people step off the cruise ships, the streets throng with people. Traffic slows and locals allow extra time to drive across town, alert for pedestrians too absorbed in sightseeing to pay attention to crossings.

All the while, regular life continues, driven by the steady metronome of the seasons.

Sitka is home to about 9,000 people. Ask Sitkans what they like about the place, and they reply by describing the slow pace of life, the advantages of living in a small town with good schools, the beauty of their surroundings. About 20 percent of the population is Alaska Native, mostly Tlingit Indians with ancestral ties to the region. Sitka is adopted quickly by its transplants, most of whom are loathe to leave. It's not unusual to find people who arrived with no plans to stay, but put down roots and raised children who are now starting families of their own.

So what do Sitkans do? For their livelihoods, they fish for salmon, halibut, black cod, crab and herring. They teach in public schools and colleges located here, and they work in medicine and government. They hire out as fishing and tour guides and drive visitors around in their boats.

Just as they work, they play. "You don't suffer from a lack of stuff to do," asserts Frank Sutton, who came to Sitka 24 years ago from Oklahoma as a pharmacist and now is director of hospital services at the regional Native hospital. "Plus, our winters aren't harsh and severe like farther north."

Sitkans hike, they bike, they swim, they boat. They play softball in summer, basketball in winter. They garden, despite the challenges posed by Sitka's

Sitka's drinking water starts as a mountain glacier. (Dan Evans)

shallow, cool, wet soils. They routinely ride state ferries to get to neighboring towns, particularly in winter when

Cruise ships deliver 200,000 visitors to Sitka each year. (Alissa Crandall)

school sports teams travel for tournaments. The ferries ply the Inside Passage, the region's watery interstate, going where paved roads won't. They also fly Outside, to Hawaii, Seattle, Mexico and other warm, sunny spots for vacations.

Sitkans celebrate the sun. Rain is part of life in Southeast, and Sitka is no exception. From ocean mists, drizzle, steady downpours and gusty storms that wash the sky in sheets of water, they see it all, about 100 inches of it a year. "One sunny day makes up for 30 days of rain," says Rick Anderson, the city assessor. "The whole area is beautiful."

Clearly, Sitka is a resilient community.

Here in the heart of the Tongass National Forest, timber used to be a big industry. For nearly 35 years, the Alaska Pulp Corp. had been Sitka's largest private employer. About 400 people worked at the mill at Silver Bay on the edge of town, processing Tongass timber into dissolving pulp used in a variety of products including rayon, cellophane and camera film. Dozens more people worked in the forest as loggers. The trees

BELOW: *Tlingits parade on July 4th in traditional regalia. (Ernest Manewal)*

RIGHT: *Wild blueberries grow ripe for picking. (Dan Evans)*

were harvested under long-term government contracts that guaranteed a steady supply of Tongass timber at low prices. Then in 1990, responding to concerns about logging Tongass and the effects of clearcutting on wildlife habitat, as well as criticisms of the timber contracts as industry subsidies, Congress passed the Tongass Timber Reform Act.

In 1993, Alaska Pulp shut down its Sitka mill, saying that price and supply changes from Tongass reform made continued operations impossible. Negotiations to reopen the mill failed as a compromise stalemated between the company and the U.S. Forest Service, which sets the contract terms. Now the company is paying for a cleanup of the site by the state Dept. of Environmental Conservation. A group of former mill employees wants to buy the property for some yet undetermined use, once the cleanup is complete.

Indeed the complicated matter has generated much, often acrimonious, debate about the future of timber in Southeast and whether logging and timber mills are compatible with tourism and fishing, industries of increasing importance in the region. Sitkans have stood on both sides.

John J. O'Connell Bridge, the nation's first cable-stayed, girder span bridge, replaced the ferry to Japonski Island in 1972. (Ernest Manewal)

Initially, the mill closure upset many here. In addition to its jobs, the mill accounted for

20 to 33 percent of the city's property tax base, a loss still being figured into the city's operation. Some people

Downtown converges at St. Michael's Cathedral. (Dan Evans)

predicted a devastating domino effect with other business failures, a decline in school enrollments and plunging housing prices as laid-off mill workers moved away.

Little of that seems to have happened yet, although the long-term consequences of the mill's shutdown remain to be seen. The initial effects on the town obviously were mitigated in part by Sitka's diverse economy. The laid-off mill workers were temporarily buffered by receiving severance and early retirement packages, and about 100 of them learned other trades through a federally funded retraining program. Some mill workers left town, but school enrollment remained steady.

Sitka has always had a housing shortage, and property prices remain high. "A decent house could sell over the weekend," says assessor Anderson. A three-bedroom home would go for around $130,000; add another $100,000 if it's on the waterfront. Island property in the sound is also in short supply; a 1.7-acre island with a couple of good homes sold for about $800,000 in spring 1995.

In the meantime, Sitkans continue discussing new directions for their town, looking to further their community's diversity. Sitka is a well-established regional center for

A Sitka fisherman checks his nets for silver salmon.(Tom Soucek)

Floats, hooks and line reflect tools of one of Southeast's busiest fishing ports. (Ernest Manewal)

tourism, commercial fishing, education and medicine.

The Mount Edgecumbe Hospital, operated in Sitka by the Southeast Alaska Regional Health Consortium to serve mostly the Native community, has become the biggest private employer. It has steadily taken on new programs throughout the region and expanded its staff, now with about 400 employees in Sitka at its 78-bed facility. The hospital opened originally as a tuberculosis sanatorium in 1947, when the disease was widespread in Alaska.

Health care, overall, is a big industry in Sitka. The city operates a smaller hospital and nursing home, and the state's big, red-roofed Pioneer Home for Alaska senior citizens is here. There are a number of private practitioners as well.

Education is another important part of Sitka. The University of Alaska offers courses here and Sitka is home to the esteemed Sheldon Jackson College, a private institution affiliated with the Presbyterian Church. The Mount Edgecumbe High School, a state boarding

The moon rises over Crescent Harbor. (Dan Evans)

school for students from throughout Alaska, sits on a campus that's part of an old military reservation on Japonski Island, connected by bridge to downtown. These colleges and schools are in addition to the elementary schools and high school in Sitka's own school district. The state police academy is also located here.

Sometimes overlooked is the presence of the U.S. Coast Guard. About 130 people are assigned to the Coast Guard's air station on Japonski Island. The air station dispatches search and rescue helicopters throughout Southeast.

Then there is fishing.

Sitka is one of the main trolling ports in Southeast, hosting several hundred boats during the peak season. The town has two commercial fish processors, Sitka Sound Seafoods and Seafood Producers Coop., which operate freezing plants year-round, hiring extra workers in summer during the peak salmon season.

Trolling for king salmon starts in June, although kings and silvers are caught commercially throughout summer. Some of Sitka's fishermen also seine for pink and chum salmon starting in late June. Fishermen also long-line for halibut and sablefish, fisheries open year-round to permit holders. Dungeness and tanner crabs, shrimp, herring roe on kelp, and

Seiners set nets in Starrigavan Bay for herring, an important fishery. (Ernest Manewal)

Bits and Pieces

Location: West side of Baranof Island, 95 air miles southwest of Juneau, 185 air miles northwest of Ketchikan, 2 hours flying time from Seattle.

Time Zone: Alaska Standard Time; the same time as Anchorage, Fairbanks and Juneau, but one hour earlier than Seattle, i.e. 6 p.m. in Seattle is 5 p.m. in Sitka.

Area Code: The area code for Sitka, as for all of Alaska, is 907.

ZIP Code: 99835.

Daylight: June 21 (summer solstice) 17 hours, 54 minutes; December 21 (winter solstice) 6 hours, 42 minutes.

Air Temperature: August highs range from 49 to 62 degrees; January lows range from 23 to 35 degrees.

Water Temperature: August mean sea surface temperature 56 degrees; January mean sea surface temperature 44 degrees.

Precipitation: June averages 3.68 inches; October averages 14.09 inches; annual precipitation averages 94 inches.

Size: The Sitka city and borough takes in all of Baranof Island and most of Chichagof Island, covering 1,968 square miles of water, 2,881 square miles of land and 1,300 miles of shoreline. The unified city-borough boundaries extend around the southern tip of Baranof, along the island's east coast, through Tenakee Inlet on Chichagof, cutting back to the west coast at the head of Lisianski Inlet.

diving for abalone and sea cucumbers are other regional commercial fisheries that attract locals.

"A lot of them are full-time fishermen, diversified in several different fisheries to keep going year-round. The larger their boats, the farther they tend to range," says Bill Davidson, an assistant area biologist for the state. The commercial fishing vessels can be anything from 17-foot skiffs used by the sea cucumber divers to 58-foot seine boats used by salmon fishermen. Most of the salmon trollers are about 40- to 45-feet long and may go north into the Gulf of Alaska or out into the ocean 30 or so miles.

An active fleet of charter boat operators catering to Sitka's increasing number of tourists makes sport fishing and wildlife touring an alternate, thriving part of the economy. "Fishing," says Davidson, "is very important to the lifestyle around here." ∎

Telemark skiers run the slopes Mount Verstovia. (Dan Evans)

Sitka Timeline

By Joan M. Antonson

The First People and Early Explorers

Tlingits move from Stikine River area to Shee Atika. When they first come to Sitka Sound is not known, but the Kiksadi Tlingits' oral history indicates that they have a permanent village there for a number of years before Euro-Americans arrive.

1775 Don Francisco de la Bodega y Quadra, a Spanish navigator, sails the 360-foot schooner *Sonora* through the region and names a mountain San Jacinto that he describes as "of the most regular and beautiful form I have ever seen."

1778 British explorer Capt. James Cook visits Sitka Sound and names the same mountain Mount Edgecumbe.

Russian Period

1799 Russians, led by Chief Manager Alexander Baranov, construct Redoubt St. Archangel Michael, now called Old Sitka, seven miles north of Sitka. The Russians build a large warehouse, stockade, blockhouse, blacksmith shop, residence for Baranov, quarters for hunters, and a men's house.

1802 After Baranov returns to Kodiak, a group of Tlingits from Indian River and nearby Crab Apple Island, led by Chief Katlean, attack and destroy the Russian fort, and kill most of the inhabitants, 20 Russians and up to 130

Aleuts. A few Russians and Aleuts reach British and American trading ships that arrive in the harbor. Capt. James Barber of the British ship *Unicorn* holds several Tlingits captive until the Russians and 18 Aleuts captured during the attack are turned over to him. Barber delivers the survivors and news of the attack to Baranov at Kodiak in late June.

1804 Russians return with five ships and attack Castle Hill, only to find it evacuated. The Tlingits have withdrawn to a fort at the mouth of Indian River, *Shish-Kee-Nu* or "Sapling Fort," a site now in Sitka National Historical Park. Fourteen buildings enclosed by a thick log wall stand at the site. After several days of unsuccessful negotiations, a six-day battle culminates with the Russians seizing and burning the Tlingit fort. The Kiksadi flee and do not return to Sitka for some 20 years.

1804 Russians occupy Castle Hill. At the time, the hill fronted on the water. In 1968 the area to the south and west is filled so that the hill is now several hundred feet from the sea.

1808 Baranov moves the colonial capital from Kodiak to New Archangel (Sitka). Because of this decision, the Russians begin to build more permanent structures at Sitka.

1816 Russians build the original St. Michael's Russian Orthodox Church close to the ocean. It is replaced with the cathedral that is built in the center of town in 1848.

Alexander Baranov was Russian America's first governor in Sitka. (Ernest Manewal)

1821   Kiksadi Tlingits return to Sitka and settle outside the Russian stockade. The area where they live is commonly referred to as the ranche.

This view of Sitka from Japonski Island, circa 1900, shows the federal agricultural building atop Castle Hill. (E.W. Merrill Collection, Sitka National Historical Park)

1830   Ferdinand von Wrangell is appointed governor of Russian America and Elizabeth, his wife, is the first governor's wife to accompany him from Russia and live at New Archangel. She is credited with "civilizing" the frontier town. She is well-liked in Sitka, and known for visits to the sick and needy and for regularly hosting receptions and balls at the Governor's House.

1834   Russian Orthodox churchman Ivan Veniaminov, later Bishop Innocent, arrives at Sitka.

1836   Construction begins on a new Governor's House, the fourth, atop Castle Hill. It is a large two-story house, 50 by 87 feet, constructed of hewn logs painted yellow and topped with a sheet-iron roof painted red and an octagonal cupola that serves as a lighthouse for vessels entering Sitka harbor. The cupola is nearly 98 feet

above the sea. Thick carpets, a grand piano, glass doors, portraits and mirrors adorn the rooms. A large room on

Tlingits pose in front of Katlian Street clan houses, 1904. (E.W. Merrill Collection, Sitka National Historical Park)

the upper floor is used for receptions, plays, concerts, balls and billiards. Other rooms house a library, a collection of clothing from the people of the northwest coast of North America, and a display of animals. The terrace around the building has 12 cannon that command the harbor and valley. Sixty steps lead from the house to the town's main street.

1841 Ivan Veniaminov returns to Sitka as Bishop of Kamchatka, the Kuriles and the Aleutians. He leaves in 1859, is appointed Metropolitan of Moscow in 1867, and dies in 1880.

1841-1843 The Russian American Co. builds a large two-story log house for the bishop. This building still stands and in the 1970s becomes part of Sitka National Historical Park. Veniaminov opens a seminary in the house that continues to operate until 1927.

1842 The Russians establish a magnetic observatory on

Japonski Island that they use until they leave Alaska in 1867.

1843 Construction begins on the Cathedral of St. Michael Archangel and

This view shows Katlian Street today, from ANB Harbor. (Dan Evans)

is completed in 1848. Veniaminov makes the clock that is on the front of the cathedral.

1852 Russians sell ice in California. They create Swan Lake, known to them as Labaishia Lake, from a low swamp, and cut blocks of ice from the lake. The first season they sold the ice for $75 per ton and shipped 250 tons. In subsequent seasons the price was substantially lower.

Early American Period

1867 On the afternoon of October 18, the official ceremony transferring ownership of Alaska from Russia to the United States takes place in front of the castle. Brig. Gen. Lovell H. Rousseau, representing the United States, and Alexei Pestchouroff, Commissioner of the Czar of Russia, meet at the flagstaff in front of the Governor's House. The Russian flag is lowered, the United States flag is raised, and a brief exchange of statements and gun salutes completes the transfer of 586,412 square miles of land. It is the first United States expansion into non-contiguous territory.

Sheldon Jackson College students pose with totems in newly created park circa 1905. (E.W. Merrill Collection, Sitka National Historical Park)

Sitka sits amid the world's largest temperate rain forest. (Ernest Manewal)

1867 Brevet Maj. Gen. Jefferson C. Davis, commander of U.S. troops in Alaska, establishes headquarters of the Military District of Alaska in the former Governor's House. Although the commanding officer does not live at the house after 1870, it continues to be the scene of Army operations in Alaska until 1877.

1869 William H. Seward, who as secretary of state negotiated the purchase of Alaska from Russia, visits Southeast Alaska

1870 Lady Jane Franklin, accompanied by Sophia Cracroft, her niece, spends a month at Sitka seeking information about Sir John Franklin who had not returned from his arctic expedition in 1848. Lady Franklin is 80 at the time of her visit to Sitka.

1870 The District of Alaska, created in 1867, is dissolved and the Army posts in Alaska are under the district headquartered at Vancouver Barracks in Washington.

1871 First attempts at hardrock gold mining made in Sitka area. Discovery in 1872 of gold-bearing quartz near head of Silver Bay spurs small rush.

1877 Army troops leave Sitka.

1878 The Cutter Packing Co. opens one of the first two salmon canneries in Alaska at Starrigavan Bay near

the first Russian fort site. Native fishermen supply the fish and most of work at the cannery is done by a

A time exposure shows a jet trail into Sitka airport, Japonski Island. (Dan Evans)

Chinese crew. The cannery makes only two small packs before it closes. It would be 39 years before another cannery opens at Sitka.

1878 Presbyterian missionaries, including John G. Brady, who would later become governor of Alaska, start missionary work at Sitka. In 1879 Brady brings his friend, Alonzo E. Austin, to Sitka. Austin opens a day school, then a boarding school for boys. He calls it the Sitka Industrial and Training School, then changes its name to Sheldon Jackson Institute. Today it is Sheldon Jackson College.

1879 White residents at Sitka request the government to send troops to protect them from the restive Natives after the loss of five Sitka Tlingit hunters from a schooner in the Bering Sea. The HMS *Osprey*, a British ship, arrives at Sitka before an American ship and finds all calm. Nonetheless, the U.S. Navy reconditions the USS *Jamestown* and assigns the Navy to Sitka.

Until the First Organic Act is passed in 1884, the Navy is assigned to protect the lives and property of residents in Alaska. The Navy stays at Sitka until 1912. The Navy hires at $18 a month about 20 Natives as crew members, First Class Boys, the first U.S. military service by Alaska Natives.

1879 Gold mining in Silver Bay prompts George Pilz to build a 10-stamp mill to process ore, the first in Alaska.

1881 The U.S. Army Signal Corps establishes a weather station at Sitka. John J. McLean is the first observer. Fred W. Fickett, who would accompany Lt. Henry T. Allen on his expedition in 1885, is the second observer. McLean returns in 1884 and remains at the station until it is closed in fall 1887.

1882 Lt. George Thornton Emmons arrives at Sitka with the U.S. Navy. For the next 17 years he mostly lives at Sitka, and he studies and writes about Tlingit culture and collects Native artifacts for various museums. His house at the corner of Lincoln and Baranof streets is the first house at Sitka with an interior finish of lath and plaster. The house is on the National Register of Historic Places.

1884 The First Organic Act designates Sitka the seat of government for the reinstated District of Alaska. The Civil Code of 1900 names Juneau as the capital, but the actual move does not take place until 1906.

1884 William R. Mills arrives in Sitka. His wife and children join him later. In time, they develop a large mercantile business, own a sawmill and Sitka's principal wharf, establish the town's water and electrical utilities, own a cold storage plant, and found the town's first bank.

1887 The Society of Alaskan Natural History and Ethnology is founded at urging of Sheldon Jackson to establish a museum.

1890 President Benjamin Harrison sets aside the historic site of the Tlingit fort at the mouth of Indian River for a public park. In 1910 it is named Sitka National Monument. Harrison's executive order in 1890 also creates a military and naval cemetery, which is today Sitka National Cemetery, and reserves Japonski Island for military purposes.

1893 Sitka residents successfully petition President Harrison for money to restore the Russian Governor's House for use by the District Court. The work is completed in September 1893, only to have the building reduced to ashes by a fire in March 1894.

1896 Bishop Peter Trimble Rowe arrives at Sitka to establish the Alaska Episcopal mission. St. Peter's By-the-Sea Church is built in 1899 and the See House for the bishop in 1905.

1898 The U.S. Department of Agriculture establishes an experimental station at Sitka headed by Dr. Charles C. Georgeson. In 1900 the department constructs a two-story building on Castle Hill that serves as headquarters for its activities in Alaska until 1932. The building stands until 1955.

1902 The U.S. Navy establishes a coaling station on Japonski Island.

1903 The only court-ordered execution in Sitka's history occurs on March 3 when Homer Bird is hung in the coal house that stands on the wharf at the end of Lincoln Street. The crime for which he is executed is a shooting near Camp Dewey on the Yukon River five years earlier. To the end he maintains that he is innocent of murder.

1905 Totems sent to the St. Louis Exposition return to Alaska and are displayed at Sitka National Monument. Artist, photographer and Sitka resident E.W. Merrill supervises placement of the totems along Totem Walk (also known as Lovers Lane).

1905 Sitka commerce is stimulated by revival of mining in the region for gold and gypsum.

1906   The capital of the District of Alaska moves from Sitka to Juneau. The move has been legislated by the Civil Code passed by Congress in 1900, but Gov. John G. Brady has not moved his offices.

1911   A new Sheldon Jackson Museum is built of concrete to replace the old wooden one and to protect the collection of Eskimo and Indian artifacts.

1912   Twelve Tlingits and a Tsimshian found the Alaska Native Brotherhood, a fraternal organization, with the encouragement of the Presbyterian Church. The group forms to fight for citizenship rights and equal treatment. The building used by the organization's Camp No. 1 in Sitka is a National Historic Landmark. A companion organization, the Alaska Native Sisterhood, organizes several years later.

Modern Sitka Emerges

1913   At a special election held on Nov. 4 residents decide to incorporate the City of Sitka as a second class city. It is the first election in which women can vote. In 1921 Sitka becomes a first class municipality.

1913   The first Territorial Legislature passes an old age pension act and creates the Pioneer Home to provide care and comfort for early settlers and pioneers of Alaska who had reached retirement age. The first home is in the old Marine barracks

Tlingit Martin White, circa 1900, wears the Bear Shirt, now at the Sitka historical park. White was the shirt's first caretaker. (Sitka National Historical Park)

building. The Pioneer Home on the site today is built in 1934-1935 and enlarged in 1956.

1913 A cold storage plant opens in Sitka and soon ranks as the

An air taxi delivers visitors to Kruzof Island. (Dan Evans)

second largest fish freezer in Alaska. It is a major factor in Sitka's economy until the buildings burn in 1973. Sitka continues as the center for outer coast fisheries, mainly black cod, salmon and halibut.

This totem detail is from the Yaadaas Crest corner pole. (Scott Chambers)

1919 The first fox farms in the area are established on many of the small islands around Sitka. Most close when fur prices drop during the Great Depression.

1923 Sitka public library opens.

1939 The Civilian Conservation Corps (CCC) employs Tlingit carver George Benson and nine other Natives to repair and restore many of the totem poles and carve reproductions of others at Sitka National Historical Park. The crew makes all of the tools used for the project by hand. At the site of the first post, known as Old Sitka, a CCC crew conducts archaeological excavations. Among the artifacts is a bronze double-headed eagle crest.

1939 The U.S. Navy establishes an air station at Sitka to patrol Southeast Alaska and the Gulf of Alaska. Seaplane facilities had been installed at Sitka two years earlier.

1941 The U.S. Army opens Fort Ray to protect the naval air station. Coastal defenses are built on several of the islands around Japonski Island, and are named Fort Rousseau.

A flower garden blooms on Merrill Street. (Ernest Manewal)

1947 The Bureau of Indian Affairs (BIA) opens Mount Edgecumbe Boarding School for up to 600 students in the naval air station buildings. They operate the school until 1983.

1949 The Prospector statue that stands outside the Sitka Pioneer Home is unveiled.

1950 The U.S. Public Health Service opens a 200-bed tuberculosis hospital on Japonski Island.

1955 Castle Hill is designated a Territorial Park by Gov. Frank Heintzleman. For the Alaska Purchase Centennial in 1967 the site is landscaped. A stone parapet with space for six Russian cannon, pilasters for six interpretive plaques, and flag poles are installed. Every Oct. 18, Sitka residents commemorate the 1867 transfer ceremony at Castle Hill as part of their Alaska Day festivities.

1959 Alaska Lumber and Pulp Co., Japanese-owned, opens a pulp mill at Sitka. The mill employs approximately 500 people and Sitka's population increases by 64 percent.

1959 Alaska Coastal Airlines of Juneau announces daily direct flights between Sitka and Annette Island where passengers can connect with north- and southbound flights of Pan American and Pacific Northern Airways.

1960 The new state of Alaska establishes its Public Safety Academy at Sitka.

1962 The Board of Indian Arts and Crafts, U.S. Department of the Interior, establishes a Native arts program at Sitka. In 1969 the Southeast Alaska Indian Cultural Center, managed by the Sitka Alaska Native Brotherhood Camp, succeeds the first program.

1965 Japonski Island airfield is constructed. Commercial use of the field starts in 1966 and the first jet lands in March 1967.

1966 St. Michael's Cathedral, the Lutheran Church, 17 businesses and more than 50 apartments in downtown Sitka burn. Because measured drawings of the church have been made, it is possible to reconstruct the Russian Orthodox cathedral. It is consecrated in 1976.

1972 A steel bridge connects Japonski Island and Sitka.

1985 The state of Alaska opens Mount Edgecumbe High School in buildings transferred from BIA.

1993 Sitka pulp mill closes.

1994-today Sitka continues expanding its role in Southeast as an important educational, medical, business and cultural center with one of the busiest commercial fishing ports in the region. More than 200,000 people visit this historic, picturesque city each year. ■

Sunbathers flock to Sandy Beach, Halibut Point Road. (Dan Evans)

Sitka by Foot

Travel the centuries in an easy walk through Sitka. Dip into Native, Russian and American history, stretch your legs in the fresh air, take in another view of the ocean. It's a perfect town for that. Most of Sitka's significant Native and Russian sites, along with an array of interesting shops, can be reached by foot. The time it takes, of course, depends on how long you spend at each stop. Fair warning: You could spend hours at any number of these places.

[**Editor's note:** Numbers in red boxes refer to locations on the street map, opposite.]

Summer flowers brighten a downtown intersection at Lincoln and Katlian streets. (Harry M. Walker)

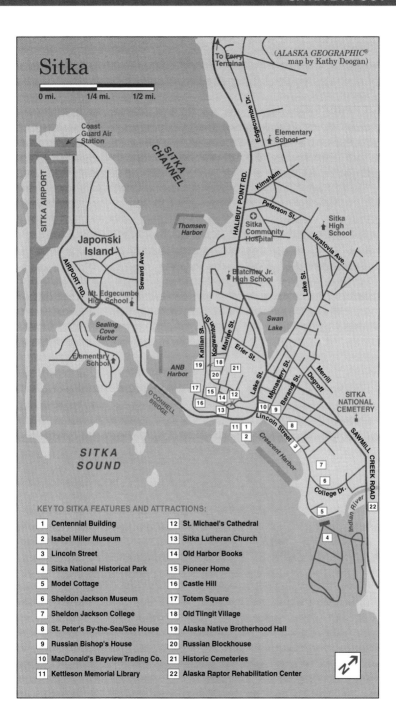

Sitka

(ALASKA GEOGRAPHIC® map by Kathy Doogan)

0 mi.   1/4 mi.   1/2 mi.

KEY TO SITKA FEATURES AND ATTRACTIONS:

1	Centennial Building	12	St. Michael's Cathedral
2	Isabel Miller Museum	13	Sitka Lutheran Church
3	Lincoln Street	14	Old Harbor Books
4	Sitka National Historical Park	15	Pioneer Home
5	Model Cottage	16	Castle Hill
6	Sheldon Jackson Museum	17	Totem Square
7	Sheldon Jackson College	18	Old Tlingit Village
8	St. Peter's By-the-Sea/See House	19	Alaska Native Brotherhood Hall
9	Russian Bishop's House	20	Russian Blockhouse
10	MacDonald's Bayview Trading Co.	21	Historic Cemeteries
11	Kettleson Memorial Library	22	Alaska Raptor Rehabilitation Center

Map labels:

To Ferry Terminal
Coast Guard Air Station
SITKA CHANNEL
SITKA AIRPORT
Edgecumbe Dr.
Elementary School
Kimsham
HALIBUT POINT RD.
Peterson St.
Sitka High School
Japonski Island
Thomsen Harbor
Sitka Community Hospital
Verstovia Ave.
AIRPORT RD.
Seward Ave.
Mt. Edgecumbe High School
Blatchley Jr. High School
Lake St.
Sealing Cove Harbor
Swan Lake
Elementary School
Katlian St.
Kogwanton St.
Marine St.
Erler St.
ANB Harbor
O'CONNELL BRIDGE
Lake St.
Monastery St.
Baranof St.
Degroff
Merrill
SITKA NATIONAL CEMETERY
Lincoln Street
Crescent Harbor
SITKA SOUND
SAWMILL CREEK ROAD
Indian River
College Dr.

Sitka Rose

If you stop and smell the roses in Sitka, it's likely you'll be sniffing the town's aromatic namesake – the Sitka Rose.

This fragrant rose shrub grows all around Sitka, as well as many other places in Alaska, popular with northern gardeners because of its showy beauty, scent and hardiness to cold.

Summer brings on a profusion of Sitka rose blooms, with one of the finest displays in rose hedges bordering the Pioneer Home. The hedges along Lincoln and Katlian streets burst forth with purplish red and pink blooms in July through August. The petals make a wonderfully perfumed potpourri. Rose hips, the fleshy red fruits that ripen after the petals fall, are picked by locals for a variety of uses, from teas to jellies.

Sitka rose, Rosa rugosa.
(Ernest Manewal)

Although these cultivars are commonly known in Alaska as Sitka roses, they are actually *Rosa rugosa*, a type of ancient wild rose native to Japan, Korea and China. Along with being the hardiest known rose, rugosas are resistant to salt, enabling them to thrive along ocean coastlines. The rugosa was introduced to the United States about 1872, according to Philip Gardner in *The Alaska Rose*, a publication of The Rose Society.

The rugosa has been hybridized extensively and today, hundreds of varieties of rugosa roses are available, ranging in color from white to deep red, with single and double blooms. They are particularly popular in climates too cold for growing tea and grandiflora roses, the showpieces of southern gardens.

So how did the rugosa become known in Alaska as the Sitka rose?

Several stories tell of its origin here, all more romantic than apparently true. Among the folklore: Prince Dmitrii Maksoutoff, the last Russian America governor, brought a rose rootstock from Russia to plant on the grave of his first wife buried in Sitka; a priest brought the rose to Sitka from his church in Russia; and, a sailing captain en route from Asia left the rose as a gift for his Sitka host.

More likely, the Sitka rose took root at Alaska's first federal agricultural experiment station in Sitka, according to Alaska gardening expert and author Lenore Hedla, of Anchorage.

The Sitka station, established in 1898 by agricultural agent Charles C. Georgeson, specialized in horticultural crop research and served as headquarters for stations that opened subsequently in Kenai, Kodiak, Rampart, Palmer and Fairbanks. Georgeson, most probably, brought the hardy rugosa roses to Sitka for plant trials. Researchers at the station would distribute seeds and plants to homesteaders, miners, loggers and anyone else who agreed to plant them and report back how they did. They did that as well with the roses, and the people who received them started using the name "Sitka rose."

The name is still commonly used today in Alaska for all colors of rugosas, although it usually denotes the pink and red varieties, which are the most commonly grown. "There are arguments about whether it's the single or double pink. But they're all called Sitka roses," says Hedla. "You know, the only place it's called a Sitka rose is in Alaska."

The rugosa, which means wrinkled, is distinguished by its handsome, dark green – and wrinkled – foliage and prickly stems, different from wild Alaska roses, including the Nootka rose, *Rosa nutkana*, which has smaller, smooth leaves spaced farther apart on more rambling, spiny brambles.

The rugosa rose was not the only plant to be closely identified with Sitka.

Experiment station researchers also produced the Sitka hybrid strawberry, by crossing Alaska's native mountain strawberry with known strawberry cultivars of the time. The wild strawberry produces tasty berries, although tiny – hardly bigger than your little fingernail and it takes lots of these wild berries to make anything. The Sitka hybrid – a larger berry, pale salmon in color but with a marvelous taste – was sent out, like the rose, to Alaskans to grow and test.

Through the years, other strawberry hybrids specific to Alaska have been introduced – the Matared, Susitna and Toklat being the most popular today. Yet they all trace back to the parent Sitka hybrid for hardiness and flavor. And today, the Sitka hybrid strawberry is sold by garden centers as an inexpensive, hardy ground cover.

The 240-acre experimental farm at Sitka was eventually closed, when the research program was turned over to the Alaska Agricultural College and School of Mines, predecessor to the University of Alaska. The Sitka rose and the Sitka hybrid strawberry continue to be enjoyed and appreciated, fragrant and flavorful legacies of this period of Sitka's history.

1 Centennial Building

A logical place to start is the Centennial Building, 330 Harbor Drive, located on the promenade at the west end of Crescent Harbor. You can pick up information and brochures about places to see and things to do in Sitka from the Visitor's Information Booth inside.

The Centennial Building, built in 1967 during the Alaska Purchase Centennial celebration, serves as a community civic and convention center. You may be able to catch special events, such as concerts of the Summer Music Festival, staged in the auditorium with picture windows overlooking the ocean. The New Archangel Dancers perform traditional Russian, Ukrainian and Moldovian folk dances almost daily during summer. Admission to the performances is $6; show times are posted weekly. Two Native dance groups also perform regularly here. The Gajaa Heen Dancers and the Noow Tlein Dancers demonstrate traditional Tlingit songs and dances passed down from elders. Admission to these performances is $5. Artworks are displayed in the building's public gallery, and locally produced arts and crafts are offered for sale during the summer. A statue of Alexander Baranov stands outside the building, which is usually open 8 a.m. to 10 p.m., Monday through Saturday in summer, and daily when cruise ships are in port.

The all-female New Archangel Dancers perform traditional Russian dances. (Ernest Manewal)

Isabel Miller

In 1963, Isabel Miller arrived in Sitka to teach sociology at Sheldon Jackson College. In the years that followed, she became practically an institution herself, administering aid to needy families as a full-time social worker, instigating the establish-

ment of Sitka's first day care center, and being active in the Presbyterian Church and many local and statewide philanthropic, civic and historical groups.

In 1983 at age 79, Miss Miller was honored publicly for her many contributions when the city museum was named after her.

Originally from Indiana, Miss Miller taught in Presbyterian mission schools in North Carolina and Arizona before coming to Alaska to be administrator of the mission school in Haines. After earning a master's degree in social services, she became a child welfare worker for the territory. Based first in Nome and then Juneau, she traveled to villages by plane, boat

Isabel Miller sparked formation of Sitka's history museum. (Artist, Pat Fager, Sitka Historical Society)

and dog sled. After a short stint in Juneau in private practice, she took the teaching position in Sitka.

She retired in 1975, in time to help the Sitka Historical Society start a local history museum. She died in 1991 at the Sitka Pioneer Home.

2 | Isabel Miller Museum

The Centennial Building also houses the Sitka Chamber of Commerce, Sitka Historical Society and the Isabel Miller Museum, a local history museum operated by the historical society. The recently refurbished museum is packed with original items from Sitka's past. The collection includes exhibits of Russian America; the tourist

(continued on page 44)

Sitka National Historical Park

Perhaps the best way to grasp the essence of premodern Sitka and the powerful spirit of Baranof Island is to stroll through the tall conifers along the trails of Sitka National Historical Park. As you hear the waves lap the shores and the gulls screech at one another, you forget that you are in modern Sitka as it approaches the end of a millennium. Instead, you see totems — those tree-high, carved markers which tell of Southeast Alaska's Native people — that follow you as you approach the end of a tiny peninsula between Sitka Sound and the mouth of the Indian River. Here archaeologists have uncovered the site of a Tlingit fort, from which warriors controlled the sound until that day in 1804 when Alexander Baranov returned with armed troops and the Russian gunship *Neva* to make the Tlingits pay for overrunning his post at Redoubt St. Michael two years earlier.

The Battle of Sitka

Baranov lost no time in attacking the Tlingits. When he had destroyed their village at what would later be called Castle Hill, he turned his guns on the Tlingit fort in what is sometimes called the Battle of Sitka. After days of fighting, the Tlingits faded into the deep forest beyond the river, leaving their spirits to roam the quiet trails.

Totems mark the entrance to the Sitka National Historical Park visitor center. (Scott Chambers)

In 1910, 106 years after the battle, Sitka National Monument was established to commemorate the battle and to protect the site of the fort. Today the monument has been incorporated into 107-acre Sitka National Historical Park. The Russian Bishop's House and the Russian blockhouse were subsequently brought under park management. See page 50 for information on the Russian Bishop's House, page 58 for the Russian blockhouse.

Totem Park

Visitors are irresistibly drawn to the park's totems. Anthropologists do not yet have enough information to know exactly their purpose or how to read them, but they do know that totem poles lined the fronts of Indian communities along the British Columbia coast and in extreme southern Southeast Alaska. Farther north, the totems were carved on houseposts in Tlingit villages. Before 1830, houseposts were more common than single poles, like those at Sitka.

Tlingit and Haida villagers of Prince of Wales Island, south of Baranof Island, donated the Sitka poles to the people of Alaska through Alaska District Gov. John G. Brady for the Alaska Exhibit at the 1904 Louisiana Purchase Exposition in St. Louis. Congress gave Alaska $50,000 to stage the exhibit, with which Brady hoped to attract visitors, and perhaps new settlers. The following year the poles were displayed in the Alaska Exhibit at the Lewis and Clark Exposition in Portland, Ore.

This detail is from the Bicentennial totem carved by Duane Pasco in 1976. (Scott Chambers)

The totem poles were then returned to Sitka, where they have captured the attention of visitors and residents ever since. A final pole, commissioned in 1976 to mark the nation's 200th anniversary, was carved by Duane Pasco and added to the earlier collection. In 1996 the park is due to add another pole to its collection, one that commemorates the history of Native people of the area.

Totem poles usually have one of four purposes: to honor a

particular family's ancestry by displaying its crest, to record a clan's history, to tell a legend or commemorate an actual event, or to memorialize a certain individual. Artisans from an opposite clan carve the pole according to specific instructions from the clan commissioning the work. The totems were painted traditionally in black, red and blue, with the colors coming from pulverized minerals. Chewed salmon eggs and saliva held the material together. Most contemporary carvers rely on commercial paints.

Time and weather have weakened the exhibit poles and they have undergone periodic restoration. By 1995, no pre-1904 poles were still in place among the 18 totems and houseposts in the park. Some of the poles have been removed. The Yaadaas crest pole was taken down in 1994 and is being treated by wood conservators. This and other poles may be displayed indoors in the future if the park's plans for an enhanced visitor center are approved.

The Park's Visitor Center

The visitor center expands on the theme of the Native people of the Sitka area. The most extensive collection represents the Kiksadi Tlingit and includes Chief Katlean's hammer. Items from other Tlingit groups and Haida and Tsimshian Indians round out the exhibits: feast poles, potlatch items, wood carvings of panting wolf, sleeping man and frog; wolf and eagle houseposts; a Tlingit housefront; a Tlingit ceremonial bear shirt and staff and a colorful Chilkat robe. Berry baskets, spruce-root baskets and a series of photos on basket construction portray some of the utilitarian aspects of the traditional Southeast Native lifestyle, and balance nicely with a series of copper pieces that the Tlingits used as money.

The word "totem" comes from the Algonquin Indians, who referred to images of family crests depicted as natural objects or animals as totems. A totem can be either an individual crest or carving, or the entire pole.

The park's staff offer slide shows on the Tlingits, the Battle of Sitka and the Russian period. They also have videos on individual totems that the public may check out. A gift shop at the center offers books on the Tlingits, the Russians and the battle, as well as locally crafted items.

In the summer, the visitor center is open 8 a.m. to 5 p.m. daily; winter hours are 8 a.m. to 5 p.m. Monday through Friday, and on weekends by arrangement. From May 1 to Sept. 30, interpretative staff offer guided tours of the nature trails and fort site. In winter, tours are offered a couple days a week or by appointment. There

is no charge to visit the park.

For more information on Sitka National Historical Park, write the Superintendent, Sitka National Historical Park, 106 Metlakatla or P.O. Box 738, Sitka,

Forest trails lead to totems at Sitka National Historical Park. (Harry M. Walker)

or call (907) 747-6281.

tradition since the late 1800s; displays about fishing and logging, tracing the development and importance of these industries in the area; and a furbished Victorian parlor with period furniture and items from early Sitka. A museum highlight is a large diorama with exacting detail that shows Sitka in 1867. The museum recently acquired a scale model of St. Michael's Cathedral as it looked in 1869. The museum, which also operates a gift shop, is open daily in summer, Tuesday through Saturday only in winter and by appointment. Call (907) 747-6588 for hours. A $1 donation is appreciated, and donors receive a souvenir Russian ruble.

3 Lincoln Street

Many interesting pieces of Sitka's history can be found along Lincoln Street, the main downtown boulevard that fronts the water from Crescent Harbor to the east.

The most genteel appearing section of Sitka may well be parallel to Lincoln along the waterfront where the street is banked by wide grassy lawns, well-kept homes and a city park. A footpath passes through the park along the harbor, alongside shade trees and benches overlooking the docks and a set of tennis courts. Continuing east on Lincoln, you'll find access to the beach.

Sheldon Jackson Museum was the first museum in Alaska. (Harry M. Walker)

This Tlingit octopus bag and Eskimo mask are part of the collection at Sheldon Jackson Museum. (Both, Ernest Manewal)

4 Sitka National Historical Park

From the harbor, follow the footpath or take Lincoln Street east about a mile where it becomes Metlakatla Street near the entrance to the 107-acre Sitka National Historical Park (see page 40). The park alone is a wonderful place to spend a day, with its museum, Native artists' studios (see Southeast Alaska Indian Cultural Center, page 60), trails through acres of forests with totem poles locally known as Totem Park, and its driftwood-covered beach for walking and sitting.

5 Model Cottage

While at this end of town, you may want to find the Model Cottage at 105 Metlakatla Street. It's the only surviving example of early American-style homes built by Natives in Sitka during the 1880s and early 1890s, part of the Presbyterian mission's efforts to acculturate the island's indigenous people. Eight cottages of this type were built on Metlakatla and Kelly streets by Native men, graduates of the Sitka Industrial and Training School, with money from a revolving loan fund set up by the mission, according to Alison Hoagland in *Buildings of Alaska* (1993).

(continued on page 48)

Sheldon Jackson

Presbyterian leader Sheldon Jackson was overseeing church mission work in the western U. S. territories in 1877 when he read a worrisome letter out of newly acquired Alaska. The letter, from an Army private at Fort Wrangell, sent Jackson's life in a new direction, triggering many changes for Alaska's indigenous people. The private wanted to know why no Christian education was available to the Tlingit Indians at Fort Wrangell.

Jackson, a zealous missionary, knew he had to do something. "The knowledge of any place that lacked the preaching of the Gospel and the ministration of the Christian Church was to him an irresistible appeal," writes Hermann Morse in *Sons of the Prophets* (1963). "The text by which he lived...and from which he often preached – was Moses' command to the people of Israel: 'Begin to possess, that thou mayest inherit the land.'"

Within a few days, Jackson boarded a steamer bound for Alaska. He was accompanied by a female missionary, who would run the school at Fort Wrangell. They arrived in August. In 1879 Jackson spent some time traveling by canoe, meeting various groups of Indians. Jackson was distressed to learn that the Army was withdrawing from Alaska, leaving the territory unpoliced. He returned to his church mission office in Denver and launched a campaign, traveling between Washington, D.C. and Alaska, to awaken the government to the needs he saw in Alaska. In the meantime, he brought missionary John G. Brady to Sitka to open a school.

Sheldon Jackson founded the first mission school and first museum in Alaska. (Alaska State Library, photo number PCA 45-1316)

The Sitka Industrial and Training School held its first classes in old Army barracks in 1878. In 1882 after a devastating fire, Jackson salvaged lumber from an abandoned cannery and directed construction of a new school building on the site of today's Sheldon Jackson College. In 1884, he was appointed as the Sitka missionary and organized a Presbyterian church congregation.

The next year, Jackson stepped into a government post as General Agent of Education for the district of Alaska. His job: To see to the education of Alaska children. Congress had allotted $25,000 for that purpose. Alaska was vast, he soon saw as he traveled along the northern coast in the revenue cutter *Bear*. He stretched the money by appealing to church leaders of other denominations to send missionaries to Alaska, suggesting specific areas where they might open schools and churches. This brought the Moravians to Bethel, the Episcopalians to Tanana, and the Quakers to Kotzebue, among others. Some criticized Dr. Jackson's methods, which included using some government money to support the mission schools. By 1892, 17 government schools and 14 church schools were operating throughout Alaska.

During this time, Jackson traveled extensively setting up and inspecting schools. Just as he advocated that Alaska's Natives learn English and adopt western ways, he also collected many outstanding examples of their culture. Writing to a friend in 1893, he explained the importance of his collections: "...in a few years there would be nothing left to show the coming generations of natives how their fathers lived." He organized the first ethnographic society at Sitka, and in 1889 built Alaska's first museum at Sitka – a wood structure in the fashion of a Tlingit plank house – to house his Native artifacts and other items of historical significance.

Jackson also initiated reindeer herding in western Alaska as a way to stabilize food supplies. Commercial whalers and fur hunters had depleted the numbers of sea mammals, which the region's Eskimos needed for food and other uses. Jackson raised money from private sources to buy and ship reindeer to Alaska from Siberia. Between 1891 and 1902, nearly 1,300 deer were imported, most to the Seward Peninsula. During this time, Jackson made 33 trips to Siberia. The herds were managed by missionary groups and herded by imported Siberians and, later, Lapps. Alaska's Eskimos apprenticed with the herders; in exchange they were given reindeer to start their own herds.

In 1897, Jackson sailed on a steamer up the Yukon River to Dawson City, Canada, exploring the river for missionary work and evaluating the land's agricultural potential for the government. Then he went to Lapland at the government's request to bring back reindeer and herders for a relief mission to starving gold miners in the upper Yukon River valley.

In 1902, he made his final and 26th trip to Alaska. Due to health problems, Jackson spent the last several years of his life working out of his General Agent office in Washington, D.C., before retiring in 1908. He died the next year at age 75.

6 | Sheldon Jackson Museum

As you walk back toward town, you'll find the dark brown Sheldon Jackson Museum near the intersection of Lincoln Street and College Drive, on the southeast edge of the Sheldon Jackson College campus. The museum houses a superb collection of Indian, Eskimo and Aleut artifacts representing the Native cultures of Alaska. Most of the objects predate the 1930s; most were collected in the 1880s and 1890s by Presbyterian missionary Sheldon Jackson. (See page 46 for more about Sheldon Jackson.)

The museum can take hours to fully explore, but items of particular interest to many visitors include the Eskimo mask collection; Katlean's helmet; the skin-covered Aleut and Eskimo kayaks; and a collection of original totem poles in the gallery's center. In addition to artifacts displayed in the glass cases, a wealth of others are found in cabinets or drawers around the gallery. Don't be shy about pulling them open to look.

The museum's octagonal gallery, built out of concrete in 1895, is the oldest concrete structure in Alaska. The state purchased the museum in 1983 and renovated and expanded the building with a wing for offices and workrooms. A steel-framed roof was built over the gallery's original wooden ceiling.

Hours are 8 a.m. to 5 p.m. daily during summer, mid-May through mid-September; and 10 a.m. to 4 p.m., Tuesday through Saturday in winter. General admission is $3. Tlingit, Athabaskan, Aleut and Eskimo artists demonstrate their skills during summer in the Native Artist Demonstrator Program sponsored by the non-profit Friends of Sheldon Jackson Museum; call (907) 747-8981 for times. Fine Alaska Native artworks are sold in the museum gift shop.

7 | Sheldon Jackson College

The brown-and-white buildings on the hill to the north, facing the water in an arc across a wide, grassy lawn, belong to Sheldon Jackson College, Alaska's oldest educational institution.

The college originated in 1878 as the Sitka Industrial and Training School for Native boys, founded by Presbyterian missionary John G. Brady, later an Alaska governor. After a fire in 1882 burned the school, Sheldon Jackson raised money to rebuild. By 1911, the facility was known as Sheldon

Jackson School and grew to offer vocational training, an elementary school and eventually a high school. In 1944, it became a two-year college open to non-Natives and started offering a four-year program in 1976.

In summers, the campus stays busy with Elderhostel programs and programs connected to the Sitka Summer Music Festival and Island Institute symposium. The college's Hames P.E. Center offers public hours for use of its swimming pool, racquetball court, gym and weight-lifting facilities. (See page 113 for more about swimming pools in Sitka.)

Also on campus, Stratton Library is open to the public. Information and maps for walking tours of the campus are available at a kiosk by the library or in the Armstrong Administration Building. Author James Michener stayed on campus while researching his novel *Alaska* (1988).

Across Lincoln Street from the campus is the college's salmon hatchery. Nearby, a rock known as the Blarney Stone is reputedly where Alexander Baranov, the first governor of Russian America, used to sit and think.

8 | St. Peter's By-the-Sea and the See House

Walking on toward town along the waterfront from the college, you'll pass St. Peter's By-the-Sea, 611 Lincoln, an active Episcopal church dating back to the early American period in Sitka.

This gothic-style stone-and-wood church was built in 1899 under Peter Trimble Rowe, first Episcopal bishop of Alaska who came to Sitka in 1896. Seed money of $2,000 to build the church was donated by a couple from Utica, N. Y., after they visited Sitka in 1897, and another

The gothic-style St. Peter's By-the-Sea Episcopal Church, built in 1899, overlooks the waterfront on Lincoln Street. (Harry M. Walker)

(continued on page 52)

Russian Bishop's House

Russian Orthodoxy provided the moral and spiritual foundation for a growing Sitka. And in keeping with the architecture of the times, the building housing its spiritual leaders has proved as sturdy as the religion itself. The National Park Service purchased the Russian Bishop's House in 1972, incorporated it into Sitka National Monument and reorganized the monument into Sitka National Historical Park. Then they began a 16-year project to restore the Bishop's House to period condition, the only historical building in Sitka to wear this distinction.

Visitors see the results of that effort in a tour of the Bishop's House, a short walk east on Lincoln Street from the downtown core. The two-story, Sitka-spruce-log building was in sad shape when Russian Orthodox bishops abandoned it for more modern quarters in 1969. For 127 years, following its completion in 1842, the building had sheltered the leaders of Russian Orthodoxy in Alaska. When the Russian American Co. received its second charter from Czar Alexander I in 1821, it agreed to ease the way of Orthodox missionaries posted to the New World. In Sitka this meant assigning Finnish carpenters working at the company's shipyard to build a bishop's residence. In 1841, Bishop Innocent, now St. Innocent, Evangelizer of the Aleuts and Apostle to America, moved in.

The Russian Bishop's House, completed in 1842, is operated as a museum. (Ernest Manewal)

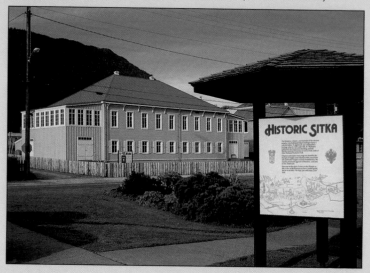

Paintings adorn the private chapel in the Russian Bishop's House. (Ernest Manewal)

The building housed more than just the bishop and his staff. Its two stories included a seminary, offices and classrooms; a kitchen, dining room, reception room and the bishop's Chapel of the Annunciation. As the youngest of the four known remaining buildings in North America dating to the Russian colonial period, the Bishop's House marked the high point in colonial architecture. Its furnishings honored the stature of its resident. And from this "ecclesiastical palace" the Bishop of Kamchatka, the Kuriles and the Aleutian Islands and his priests were responsible for a region stretching from the Kamchatka Peninsula of Russia, through Alaska and south along North America's west coast to northern California.

The Finnish shipwrights used the latest construction techniques including sand-insulated subfloors and ceilings. Linen canvas or sailcloth, painted or wallpapered, covered the walls and ceilings.

Since paper supplies had to travel thousands of miles by sea to reach Sitka, the builders readily recycled any scraps from the Diocese's memos and ledgers. This paper was cut into strips and glued together to seal cracks in the walls. For those of us passing by more than a century later, these scraps offer a treasure of historical records: maps, correspondence, menus, travel accounts.

In summer, the Russian Bishop's House is open daily from 9:30 a.m. to noon, and from l p.m. to 3 p.m.; in winter by appointment only.

$3,000 to complete the building was raised through donations. Its architecture reflected the prevailing influences of the time, a view promoted by the Cambridge Camden Society of England that gothic architecture was the best visual and spacial representation of the gospel. Bishop Rowe himself built the See House behind the church in 1905, as well as the stone wall in front. He and his wife lived here until 1912, when they moved to Seattle. After his death in 1942, his body was returned for burial in the churchyard.

The See House now holds church offices and a fellowship hall where historic photos are displayed; both the See House and the church building are open to the public.

9 | Russian Bishop's House

One of the few original Russian America buildings in Sitka is the Russian Bishop's House, at the corner of Lincoln and Monastery streets (see page 50). Today, the restored house and grounds, including a Russian garden in the front, are managed by the National Park Service.

A Sitka Princess

Princess Adelaide Ivanovna Bushman Maksoutoff was the first wife of Alaska's Russian governor, Prince Dmitrii Maksoutoff. He was the last of the 14 Russian governors in charge of Russian America, and who lived in Sitka.

At the time of the Maksoutoffs, Sitka reportedly had a population of 2,500, about 400 of whom were Russians. An assortment of wooden buildings lined the town's single dirt street. There was an Orthodox cathedral, an Indian church, a Lutheran chapel, a club, hospital and four schools. The chief entertainment for the Russians included balls and musical and theatrical performances at the governor's home.

During this time, the Russian American Co. had a fleet of 13 ships stationed at Sitka, sailing from Sitka to St. Petersburg and Canton, China, and to distant company posts in the Aleutians, at the mouth of the Yukon River, in Kodiak and near San Francisco.

The Princess died in Sitka on Dec. 19, 1862, three months after the birth of their third child. The Prince returned to Russia with his children, married a second wife and returned with his family to Sitka, where he served during the sale of Alaska to America and finally liquidated the Russian American Co.'s holdings.

10 MacDonald's Bayview Trading Co.

Tlingit designs painted on cedar adorn this Kogwanton Street house. (Harry M. Walker)

Sitka has many interesting downtown shops, eateries and galleries, including those inside the two-story MacDonald's Bayview Trading Co., 407 Lincoln. An extraordinary assortment of

St. Michael's Cathedral

The first Russian Orthodox church in Sitka was a small chapel built close to the water in 1816 and dedicated to Saint Michael. It was furnished with church articles salvaged from the ocean after the wreck of the Russian ship *Neva*. After 25 years, the chapel deteriorated and a new church, St. Michael's Cathedral, was built in the center of town. The cornerstone was laid in 1844 and the church was dedicated in 1848. It was built of thick Sitka spruce logs covered with dark gray clapboard in an architectural style found near St. Petersburg.

The copper domes of St. Michael's Cathedral mark Sitka's skyline. (Harry M. Walker)

On Jan. 2, 1966, 118 years later, fire whipped through downtown Sitka, destroying the cathedral, which had been designated a National Historic Landmark four years earlier. Vigilant townspeople were able to save many of the cathedral's icons and religious objects, some dating back to the first chapel, such as silver eucharistic vessels and vestments made with Chinese silk. Only one large painting, some church records and the bronze church bells were lost. The cathedral was rebuilt on the same site from the original blueprints, this time using fireproof construction. Its bells were recast to duplicate the originals. The new structure was consecrated in 1976.

Russian handicrafts and fine art, including a room full of painted enamel boxes, can be found at The Russian American Co. shop on the second level. The Bayview Restaurant, with tables on an upstairs patio overlooking Crescent Harbor, specializes in Russian foods, along with fresh seafoods, gourmet burgers and deli sandwiches. The building also has a postal substation and public restrooms.

11 Kettleson Memorial Library

Continuing along Harbor Drive, just west of the Centennial Building is the city's public Kettleson Memorial Library, 320 Harbor Drive. The library has a good selection of Alaskana and books about Northwest Coast Indians, including Tlingits, their art and culture. The library has a phone available at no charge for local calls, and binoculars you can use to watch through the windows for whales, seals, birds and other creatures in the sound. If you bring in a paperback in good condition, you can trade it for another; ask at the desk for the paperback exchange. The library is open every day; call for hours, (907) 747-8708. A large Tlingit canoe hand-carved from a single log is displayed under a roofed area outside between the library and Centennial Building.

12 St. Michael's Cathedral

Continue west along Harbor Drive to Maksoutoff Street and turn right, or take Harbor back to Lincoln and turn left, and you'll see the centerpiece of downtown looming ahead – St. Michael's Cathedral, with its 84-foot-tall bell tower. This historic Russian Orthodox cathedral houses a remarkable collection of icons and vestments, and its

The bronze Prospector weathers a January morning at the Pioneer Home for elderly Alaskans. (L.J. Campbell, staff)

congregation welcomes visitors. (See page 54.)

The cathedral opens noon to 4 p.m. daily in summer, with earlier hours on cruise ship days. A $1 donation is requested.

13 Sitka Lutheran Church

Another church with its roots in Russian America is the Sitka Lutheran Church, 224 Lincoln. The first non-Russian Orthodox church in Alaska, the Lutheran church was established under Russian Gov. Adolf Etolin, a Lutheran from Finland who arrived in Sitka in 1840. He brought his wife, a devout Lutheran, and a young pastor, Uno Cygnaeus, who held services, first in the Governor's House, then later in a church building dedicated at this site in 1843. That building was torn down in 1888. A congregation was re-established in 1940 and built a new church on the historic site. The current structure was rebuilt in 1966 following a fire, and renovated after a second fire in 1994. An exhibit of historic items is planned, including an 1840 pulpit, an 1844 pipe organ, communion rail and early photos.

14 Old Harbor Books

A few steps down the street is contemporary landmark Old Harbor Books, 201 Lincoln Street. The store stocks an extensive selection of books about Alaska, as well as fiction and nonfiction. U.S. Geological Survey topographic maps of the area can be purchased here, too. Behind the shop, The Back Door cafe offers espresso and pastries.

15 Pioneer Home

Continuing west on Lincoln, the massive cream-colored red-roofed Pioneer Home appears, a familiar landmark on Sitka's skyline. Established in 1913 by the first Territorial Legislature as a residence for elderly male prospectors, it started out in abandoned Navy barracks. The main part of the present building was built on the old Russian parade grounds, opening to its first 170 residents in March 1934. The home was expanded to include women pioneers with a new wing in 1956. The 13.5-foot-tall bronze statue of The Prospector in front was unveiled in 1949. Victor Alonzo Lewis, a Seattle sculptor, modeled it after pioneer William "Skagway Bill" Fonda. Handicrafts made by residents are sold in a shop in the basement. Outside, flower gardens of

Castle Hill

Long before the Russians appeared, the Kiksadi Tlingits lived on what's now known as Castle Hill, a naturally strategic vantage point overlooking the water.

After Russian occupation of Sitka in 1804, the hill held a succession of fortified buildings starting with the home of the first governor of Russian America, Alexander Baranov. In 1837, a new Governor's House was built on the hill by Gov. Ivan Kupreanov. The large, two-story building practically filled the hilltop and was capped by a lighthouse in the center of the roof. The home was surrounded by a wooden wall with about 40 cannons, mostly guns from old ships. This residence dominated Sitka's waterfront until it burned in 1894. The American's called it Baranov's Castle, although Baranov never saw it, and from this came the name Castle Hill.

Uniformed soldiers and costumed residents participate in the Alaska Day flag raising ceremony on Castle Hill. (Ernest Manewal)

perennials and some 4,000 annuals – many of which are started each spring in the home's greenhouse – grace the grounds with colorful blooms throughout the growing season. Visitors are welcome.

Russian Blockhouse

Standing facing the Pioneer Home, look left to a small knob and the Russian blockhouse rising from its top. The current blockhouse is a replica of those that guarded the stockade separating the Russian compound from the Tlingit village, or ranche, in early Sitka.

The National Park Service reconstructed the blockhouse in 1962 on land leased from the Bureau of Land Management. The structure straddles the line of the old stockade and sits on the site of Blockhouse C, demolished in the 1890s. In design, however, the current structure follows that of Blockhouse D, which stood 50 yards northeast of the stockade and was torn down in the 1920s.

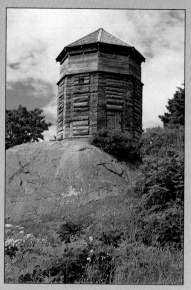

After their defeat by Alexander Baranov in 1804, the Tlingits abandoned the Sitka site. About 20 years later, they moved back near the settlement, but were not allowed inside the stockade even though the Russians depended on them for fresh food and meat to supplement the pigs they raised and food stocks off ships from Russia. They traded with the Natives in a special, protected compound that the Tlingits entered through a

The Russian blockhouse stands on a hilltop overlooking downtown Sitka. (Harry M. Walker)

portcullis door guarded by two or three Russians. Women and children did most of the trading, and Native women were paid by the Russians as spies to warn them of any upcoming hostility. The Russians feared the Tlingits and kept guns on the ranche from the stockade.

After the transfer to United States control, the U.S. Army became the official peacemakers among Natives, the remaining Russians and new settlers. The Army withdrew in 1877, and within a week the Natives tore down a portion of the stockade and it was never rebuilt.

The blockhouse is not open to the public.

16 Castle Hill

Across Lincoln from the Pioneer Home a sidewalk leads to stone steps up Castle Hill, a tiny state park and historic site with a panoramic view of the town and sound. (See page 57.) Renovations to the park include making the steep access easier for those with physical disabilities.

The ceremony transferring Alaska from Russia was held here on Oct. 18, 1867, when the American flag was raised. The transfer is celebrated each year with a week-long schedule of parties and parades with people dressed in period costumes, culminating Oct. 18 with a reenactment of the flag raising. The hill was also site of an Alaska statehood ceremony in 1959, when Gov. William Egan hoisted the first American flag to contain the 49th star, representing Alaska.

17 Totem Square

At the corner of Lincoln and Katlian streets, almost to the water, Totem Square Park holds a Russian cannon and three anchors recovered from the Sitka vicinity, probably lost by early British or American explorers. The totem pole displays the double-headed eagle, a symbol of Russian America. Across the parking lot is the Totem Square Complex, a shopping and business plaza renovated from the old Sheffield Hotel. Located here is a restaurant, an outdoor clothing, surplus and gift shop, a beauty salon, a postal substation and public restrooms.

18 Old Tlingit Village

Katlian and Kogwantan streets run north through the area that once held the old Tlingit village, the ranche, outside the Russian stockade. Katlian parallels the shoreline of Sitka Channel with Kogwantan on the hillside above. This is a picturesque working area, with docks and canneries, shops and old houses including a wooden home entirely covered on the outside with Tlingit designs.

19 Alaska Native Brotherhood Hall

The Alaska Native Brotherhood Hall stands on Katlian Street. Formed in 1912 by Tlingits to fight discrimination against Natives, the ANB was the first Native organization to wield political clout. This two-story wooden hall built in 1914 was the first ANB camp in Alaska.

Southeast Alaska Indian Cultural Center

People interested in learning more about Alaska Native art, particularly Tlingit art traditions, should visit the Southeast Alaska Indian Cultural Center, located in a wing adjacent to the Sitka historical park visitor center.

Each day during summer, artists at the center demonstrate woodcarving, silver work, beading and weaving. Four artists are paid to demonstrate their skills, interpret their work and answer questions from visitors.

Tom Joseph, a 31-year-old Tlingit woodcarver, has worked at the center as a demonstrator for five summers. In his spare time, he works on commissioned pieces, such as a totem for a new public building in Anchorage. In his role at the center, though, he produces smaller items, such as bentwood boxes and potlatch bowls. And he answers lots of questions. The most common: What kind of wood and paint are you using, and what are you making?

He uses alder and red and yellow cedar, which grow throughout Southeast. Cedar has been traditionally used by Tlingits for canoes, totems, houseposts and the like, while alder was preferred for eating

Tlingit Will Burkhart works in the wood-carving studio at the Southeast Alaska Cultural Center. Burkhart has been commissioned to create a new totem pole commemorating Sitka-area Tlingits to be erected in spring 1996 at Sitka National Historical Park. (Sitka National Historical Park)

Dave Galanin, Tlingit silver carver, works at the cultural center. (L.J. Campbell, staff)

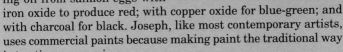

utensils and bowls because it didn't impart flavor to the food.

Early Tlingits made paints to decorate their carvings, mixing oil from salmon eggs with iron oxide to produce red; with copper oxide for blue-green; and with charcoal for black. Joseph, like most contemporary artists, uses commercial paints because making paint the traditional way is too time-consuming.

Bentwood boxes were made in a variety of sizes, depending on their intended use. To make such a box, a continuous length of wood is scored where the corners will be, then steamed until it is pliable enough to bend into shape. One of his recent works was a potlatch, or feast, bowl carved from red cedar in the shape of a frog. Such a bowl would be used during a clan gathering.

Often hundreds of visitors pass through the center daily during the tourist season in Sitka, and particularly busy days can be expected when cruise ships are in town. Joseph says he likes talking to people about his art and Tlingit culture. "It's nice when people are really interested in what's going on," he says.

The center opened about 25 years ago, sponsored by the Alaska Native Brotherhood. It recently incorporated as a separate entity. Since its start, however, it has operated in partnership with the National Park Service, which provides funding.

No artworks are sold at the cultural center, although some items produced there are available in the gift shop inside the park's visitor center.

Several of the finer galleries and shops around town carry traditional and contemporary works created by the center's demonstrators and other Alaska Native artists based in Sitka and elsewhere in the state. These include the Sheldon Jackson Museum, Sitka Rose Gallery and The Artist's Cove.

The center is open 8 a.m. to 5 p.m. every day through summer, although only one artist usually works on weekends. The center's busiest visitor days are Tuesdays, Wednesdays and Thursdays, when cruise ships are in town; travelers with more flexible schedules will find Mondays and Fridays less crowded. The artists take an hour-long lunch break, staggering their times so at least one continues demonstrating.

The center is officially closed October through April, although some artists continue using the studio space.

Bicycling

Sitka lends itself to bicycle touring with its generously wide downtown streets, relative lack of heavy truck traffic and refreshing ocean breezes.

A bike path parallels Sawmill Creek Road several miles from Jeff Davis Street out to the post office, and the path intersects trails leading through Sitka National Historical Park. There's even a bicycle race up and down Harbor Mountain on Alaska Day.

Two downtown shops rent bicycles, with helmets and locks, by the hour, day and week:

Six-speed mountain-street bike hybrids, good for around town touring, are available from Southeast Diving and Sports Shop on Lincoln Street.

Yellow Jersey Cycle Shop on Katlian Street rents out 21-speed mountain bikes, the choice for an ascent, say, of Harbor Mountain, a steep climb up a gravel road for panoramic views of the area. Prepare for a swift, switchback descent, and stay alert to cars driving the road too. "It takes about an hour to go up, 15 minutes to come down," says Bill Hughes, owner of Yellow Jersey and coordinator of the annual Alaska Day race.

A two-mile dirt road through U.S. Forest Service land to Blue Lake is another popular cycling route, as is the dirt road to Green Lake. The latter is closed to motorized traffic except city-owned maintenance vehicles.

Those itching for more remote cycling might consider trying the trails on Kruzof Island, but you need to arrange for a boat drop-off. A trail from Mud Bay, on the Sitka side of Kruzof, crosses the island to Shelikoff Bay on the outer coast where a Forest Service recreation cabin is located.

20 Russian Blockhouse

Back toward the center of town, at the corner of Marine and Kogwantan streets is a replica of a Russian blockhouse, part of the old Russian stockade. (see page 58).

21 Historic Cemeteries

Several old cemeteries are in this vicinity, too, with graves dating back into the 1840s, where men, women and children were buried far from their homeland. Topping the hill above the blockhouse is the old Russian Orthodox cemetery. The grave of Princess Maksoutoff (see page 52) is located at the end of Princess Way, near the intersection of Seward and Marine streets. Nearby is the old Lutheran cemetery and at

the end of Observatory Street
is the wooded old Russian
cemetery. ◼

*Mount Verstovia (3,300 feet) rises
behind Sitka in this view from
Japonski Island. (Ernest Manewal)*

Sitka by Road

Sitka's road system is one of the smallest of any Southeast community, but there are about 30 miles of roads, all worth exploring if you have the time, a car and are tired of hoofing it.

Sitka has car rental agencies located at the airport, as well as on Sawmill Creek and Halibut Point roads. In late 1995 gasoline ranged from $1.45 to $1.49 per gallon. If you arrive by ferry, buses meet each arrival and will take you downtown. You can catch a taxi or shuttle bus to the airport, or walk if you want the exercise. It's about a half hour walk from St. Michael's Cathedral to the airport.

Once you have a vehicle, from downtown you have two basic directions in which to drive: southeast along Sawmill Creek Road, or northwest along Halibut Point Road. There are cross streets and a grid system in downtown Sitka, but those are more easily explored on foot.

Southbound

Sawmill Creek Road runs 7.4 miles from Lake Street near Swan Lake to Silver Bay. Along the way it passes the Sitka National Cemetery, the State Trooper Academy, the Alaska Raptor Rehabilitation Center, the Post Office, Whale Park and Alaska Pulp Corp.'s inactive pulp mill. The first 5.4 miles to the bridge across Sawmill Creek are paved; a gravel road continues another 1.5 miles to Herring Cove. Public vehicle access is barred at this point even though the road proceeds to Green Lake hydroelectric plant. The road is open to bicyclists and foot traffic, but not to motorized vehicles.

The drive offers good views of some of the islands in Sitka Sound and of the saltwater lifestyle of many of the

community's residents.
Farther out from the town's
core, the road follows the
shore of the Eastern Channel
of Sitka Sound, accompanied
by entrancing views of the

*Sitka National Cemetery dates to
1867, the only national graveyard
west of the Rocky Mountains until
World War II. (Ernest Manewal)*

water and the steep, forested slopes of Baranof Island beyond.
Stop at Whale Park at mile 4, an overlook with interpretative
signs, boardwalks and gazebos with binoculars from which
you can spot humpback whales, especially in the fall, early
winter and spring, when they're feeding near town.

At the pulp mill, a gravel side road leads up the side of a
hill and on about two miles to Sawmill Creek Campground
and Blue Lake.

Another branch off Sawmill Creek Road leads up Indian
River valley. This unmarked, one-mile, gravel road begins
about 100 to 150 yards before Indian River bridge, which is
marked. The road turns toward the mountains by the State
Trooper Academy and leads to the city water pump house.
Indian River trail takes off from here.

Northbound
The other main road leading out of downtown Sitka is

Halibut Point Road, which begins at the intersection of Harbor Drive and Lincoln Street and continues nearly 8 miles to Starrigavan Campground.

A five-mile drive up Harbor Mountain offers this view. (Ernest Manewal)

Heading northwest, the route parallels Sitka Sound with numerous turnouts where you can stop to enjoy the view.

Turn in at the Sea Mart about two miles out for a snack, which you can eat in your car in the parking lot while you watch the gulls scavenging for dinner along the beach. You'll also find a picnic area with sheltered tables along the beach down a short path leading from the parking lot; it's also accessible from the highway. Pioneer Park, just down the road a bit, has a picnic and day use area as well. If you're drawn to a more rural setting, save your snack for a picnic at Halibut Point State Recreation Site at about mile 5. If cold water doesn't deter you, there's a swimming beach here.

As the road approaches the Alaska Marine Highway ferry terminal at mile 7, just beyond you can see the site of Alexander Baranov's original fort, now commemorated as Old Sitka, with interpretive signs and picnic tables. This is a great spot to relax, let your imagination drift back 200 years to the early Russian efforts, or listen to the *swoosh* of spouting whales and the cries of gulls, geese and ducks.

Mount Edgecumbe School

Mount Edgecumbe High School, located on Japonski Island, attracts young people from throughout rural Alaska. The school, Alaska's only public boarding high school, is noted for its innovative, academic curriculum. About 270 students attend each year, with nearly half going on to college and other advanced degree programs.

Mount Edgecumbe occupies buildings on Japonski constructed during World War II as a naval air station. The property was transferred after the war to the Bureau of Indian Affairs, which opened Mount Edgecumbe in 1947 to replace Wrangell Institute and Eklutna Vocational School located elsewhere in Alaska. During 36 years of BIA administration, nearly 10,000 students attended Mount Edgecumbe and more than 3,900 earned diplomas.

In 1983, BIA closed the school. The state reopened it in 1985 to all high school-aged residents, but targeted rural Native students. Classes are offered in English, math, social studies, science, physical education, social skills, computer science and Asian languages. Core classes are conducted during the day, with study halls and extracurricular activities offered after school and in evenings.

The school approaches education from a unique perspective. For instance, because Alaska's geographic location brings considerable political and trade interactions with Japan and China, the school offers Pacific Rim studies, integrated with core academic courses. As an example, students become conversational in Japanese and Chinese to meet their foreign language requirement.

The school takes a non-traditional approach, as well, to vocational education. It is taught through entrepreneurship and work-study. In one such program, the students process, package and market smoked salmon. Students traveled overseas to study market potential and developed products based on export demands.

Students at Mount Edgecumbe School come from villages throughout rural Alaska. (Ernest Manewal)

Starrigavan Creek enters salt water here. From the bridge in season you can watch the pink salmon running. The gravel Nelson Logging Road, built for use by loggers in the 1970s but no longer traveled by logging trucks, follows the south side of the creek. There is a shooting

An old tug lies on the beach of Jamestown Bay. (Dan Evans)

Sawmill Creek Road leads to the Alaska Pulp Corp. mill, inactive since 1993 after 36 years as Sitka's largest employer. (Staff)

range about 1.5 to 2 miles in. The road continues on but wash-outs and lack of maintenance make it unsuitable for most vehicles beyond the shooting range.

Across the bridge lies Starrigavan Campground and the end of Halibut Point Road. The campground is part of Starrigavan Recreation Area with boardwalks and trails, picnic shelters, a bird viewing platform and a river overlook. (See page 115 for more about this recreation area.)

Harbor Mountain Road

Just beyond mile 4 of Halibut Point Road, a gravel side road turns inland and begins a five-mile steep run up Harbor Mountain. The road ends at a parking lot, where foot trails lead higher up the mountain. (See page 72 for more about the trails.)

Originally built during World War II to serve lookout posts on Harbor Mountain, the road offers a spectacular look at Southeast's thick conifer forests and the ever-present Sitka Sound. The road is closed to cars until June each year because of snow. But if you're in Sitka in summer and you have time for only one short drive, head up Harbor Mountain. ■

Alaska Raptor Rehabilitation Center

One of Sitka's biggest attractions is the Alaska Raptor Rehabilitation Center at 1101 Sawmill Creek Road. You will be greeted by Clicker, the western screech owl, or Volta, one of several bald eagles that participate in the educational programs. The center cares for injured or ill birds, usually birds of prey, although volunteers will try to help any bird from trumpeter swans to rufous hummingbirds to chickens. The center usually has on hand several of Alaska's raptor species, including bald eagles; red-tailed hawks; great-horned, barred, short-eared, western screech and pygmy owls. Programs offer visitors a chance to see volunteers working with the birds, including teaching injured bald eagles how to fly again. The center strives to rehabilitate the animals and return them to the wild; those that cannot be released are used in educational programs or are sent to breeding facilities.

From May 15 to September 30 the center is open whenever a cruise ship is in port, usually 8 a.m. to 5 p.m. It's best to call a day ahead, (907) 747-8662, to doublecheck. The center's full program in summer includes talks and demonstrations with the birds and an 8-minute video. In winter, the facility is open 8 a.m. to 5 p.m. Monday through Friday. There is no formal program in winter but you can see the displays and the birds in their cages. Admission is charged in summer. A gift shop carries books, T-shirts, materials on rehabilitating animals and other items.

Eagles are released from the Alaska Raptor Rehabilitation Center. (Ernest Manewal)

The center, founded in 1980 and

ABOVE: *See a bald eagle up close at the Raptor Center. (Harry M. Walker)*

LEFT: *Volunteers help rehabilitate raptors, like this immature bald eagle. (Ernest Manewal)*

operated by more than 200 volunteers and seven paid staff, receives no government funding; its support comes from donations and memberships. Outdated medical supplies arrive in care pack-ages from around the country. Alaska Airlines flies injured birds free from all over Alaska to Sitka in dog kennels. Sitka residents donate fish, bear and other carcasses. Don't miss this chance to see some of the best of Sitka's wildlife, up close and personal.

Hiking Near Sitka

If you've explored Sitka by road and water and are ready for a hike, there are several maintained trails in the vicinity. For current trail conditions, check with the U.S. Forest Service Office, Katlian Street and Siginaka Way, phone (907) 747-6671. U.S. Geological Survey topographic maps are available at Old Harbor Books, White's Pharmacy and the U.S. Forest Service office on Katlian Street.

Among the most spectacular trails are those on Harbor Mountain, reached most easily from the trailhead at the parking lot at the end of Harbor Mountain Road. This road is the only one in Southeast Alaska that provides access to subalpine habitat. Steep, tight turns make the road unsuitable to vehicles pulling trailers or to recreational vehicles.

[**Editor's note:** Numbers in green boxes refer to locations on the area map, opposite.]

1 Harbor Mountain Shelter Trail

(Length one way, .1 mile; hiking time one way, 5 minutes.) Pull into the parking lot about 4.5 miles up Harbor Mountain Road. A planked trail heads northwest to a covered picnic site, passing subalpine meadows and streamlets along the way. The covered site becomes a warming shelter in winter for cross-country skiers and snow machiners when the Sitka Snowmobilers Club walls up the sides of the shelter.

2 Harbor Mountain Ridge Trail

(Length one way, 2 miles; hiking time one way, 2 hours.) This trail, with an elevation gain of 500 feet, ends at the junction with the Gavan Hill Trail, at 2,505 feet on Harbor Mountain. Some sections can be muddy, other stretches are

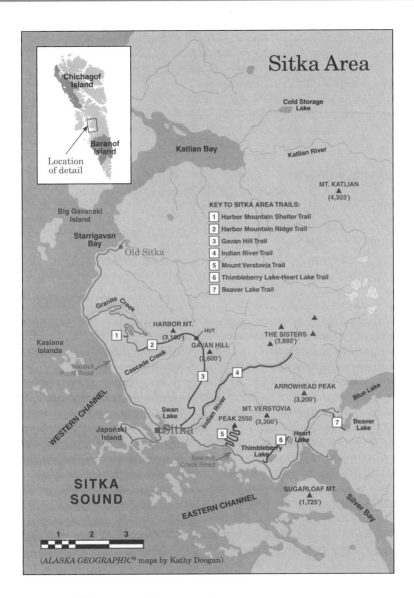

Sitka Area

Chichagof
Island

Baranof
Island

Location
of detail

Cold Storage
Lake

Katlian Bay

Katlian River

MT. KATLIAN
(4,303')

KEY TO SITKA AREA TRAILS:

Big Gavanski
Island

1 Harbor Mountain Shelter Trail

2 Harbor Mountain Ridge Trail

Starrigavan
Bay

3 Gavan Hill Trail

Old Sitka

4 Indian River Trail

5 Mount Verstovia Trail

6 Thimbleberry Lake-Heart Lake Trail

7 Beaver Lake Trail

Granite Creek

HARBOR MT.
(3,180')

HUT

THE SISTERS
(3,880')

Kasiana
Islands

1

2

GAVAN HILL
(2,600')

Halibut
Point Road

Cascade Creek

3

4

ARROWHEAD PEAK
(3,200')

Blue Lake

Swan
Lake

Indian River

MT. VERSTOVIA

PEAK 2550 (3,300')

7

Beaver
Lake

Japonski
Island

Sitka

5

6

Heart
Lake

Thimbleberry
Lake

Sawmill
Creek Road

SITKA
SOUND

SUGARLOAF MT.
(1,725')

Silver Bay

EASTERN CHANNEL

WESTERN CHANNEL

1   2   3

(ALASKA GEOGRAPHIC® maps by Kathy Doogan)

steep, and bears may be present.

Beginning at the parking lot, climb the trail marked by handrails in a series of switchbacks that gain 300 feet in elevation. At the ridge, a spur runs left to an overlook offering unforgettable views of Sitka, Sitka Sound and Mount Edgecumbe on Kruzof Island.

Harbor Mountain Ridge Trail continues along the ridge and veers to the right bypassing the ruins of a World War II observation post. Subalpine vistas dominate this portion of the trail, which runs along the side of a meadow and follows a ridge toward the peaks of Harbor Mountain. Rock cairns mark the line of travel across a rock slide. A man-made shelter indicates the end of the trail and the junction with the Gavan Hill Trail that leads back to Sitka.

3 Gavan Hill Trail

(Length one way, 3 miles; hiking time one way, 3 to 4 hours.) You can tackle this route by continuing past the hut at the end of the Harbor Mountain Ridge Trail and down the slopes of Gavan Hill to Baranof Street in Sitka, thus skipping much

A trail along Indian River cuts through the rain forest. (Ernest Manewal)

of the 2,505-foot climb. Or you can step onto the trail just past the house at 508 Baranof Street. If you do the latter, you face a long, uphill route after a half-mile or so of hiking through marshes and scrubby forests. Once up on Gavan Hill Ridge, subalpine vistas come into view. The trail climbs two peaks and ends at the Gavan/Harbor Mountain Hut shelter. Remember to watch for bears.

4 Indian River Trail

(Length one way, 5.5 miles; hiking time one way, 4 hours.) Make your way to the end of Indian River Road where the trail begins west of the pump house. This easy trail climbs gradually, is well-maintained, but can be muddy in spots, and provides an opportunity to hike through Southeast rain forest of old-growth Sitka spruce, western hemlock and yellow cedar. Open areas offer views of the Indian River valley and The Sisters Mountains. Watch for wildlife including Sitka black-tailed deer and bears. The trail ends at a waterfall near the head of the valley.

5 Mount Verstovia Trail

(Length one way, 2.5 miles; hiking time one way, 3 hours.) In contrast with Indian River Trail, this route is tough going, brushy, steep and not well-maintained. It is possible to lose the way up a series of switchbacks on the southwest side of the mountain. As always, watch for bears.

The trail begins 2 miles east of town on Sawmill Creek Road and ends at the summit of Mount Verstovia.

[**Note:** The local names for Verstovia and neighboring Arrowhead do not designate the same peaks as those shown on USGS maps. The local name Verstovia indicates Peak 2550 on USGS maps; the local name Arrowhead stands for Mount Verstovia on USGS maps.]

6 Thimbleberry Lake – Heart Lake Trail

(Length one way, .25 mile to Thimbleberry Lake, 1 mile to Heart Lake; hiking time one way, 15 minutes to 1 hour.) While lack of maintenance can leave these short trails muddy and slippery, the trails are not particularly steep and are suitable to year-round travel. Turn left off Sawmill Creek Road just beyond Thimbleberry Creek Bridge into a parking lot where the trail begins. Don't forget to watch for bears.

(continued on page 78)

Guided Tours

While Sitka is easy to navigate on your own by foot or car, you may opt for a guided tour on land, by air or water.

Land-based Tours

Prices range from $8 to $33 per person; on some tours young children are included free or at reduced prices when accompanied by adults.

New Archangel Walking Tours, P.O. Box 2626, Sitka:
■ This 1.5-hour guided walk includes the historic and modern sights of downtown. Tours start from near the visitor's dock at Crescent Harbor. Phone (907) 747-7277.

Wildlife watchers disembark from the the St. Maria. *(Dan Evans)*

Sitka Tours, P.O. Box 1001, Sitka, offers four tours:
■ The Express Tour is an hour-long bus ride through town for a show and tell, with no stops. This tour is sold at the dock when cruise ships are in town.
■ The 2.5-hour Historic Tour by bus stops at all of Sitka's historic sites with admission to a performance by the New Archangel Dancers.
■ The Raptor Tour is a longer, and slightly more costly, version of the historic tour with a stop at the Raptor Rehabilitation Center.

■ The Ferry Stopover Tour caters to ferry passengers. The 2- to 3-hour tour, which originates and ends at the ferry terminal, includes stops at the Sitka National Historical Park, St. Michael's Cathedral and the Isabel Miller Museum with some time for shopping.

Phone (907) 747-8443 for more about Sitka Tours.

Sitka Tribe of Alaska, 456 Katlian Street, Sitka:

■ This 2.5-hour tour by passenger van gives the Native perspective of historical and contemporary Sitka. Highlights include Sitka National Historical Park, Sheldon Jackson Museum, and a narrative of the old Tlingit village. Some tours include a performance of the Gajaa Heen Dancers. Phone (907) 747-3207.

Walk in the Wild Rainforest Walking Tour, P.O. Box 6057, Sitka:

■ This 3-hour natural history hike explores the rain forest on the outskirts of Sitka. Van delivery to the trailhead is provided. Phone (907) 747-3530.

Flightseeing Tours

Prices start at $85 per person per hour.

Seaborne Seaplane Adventures, P.O. Box 6440, Ketchikan 99901:

■ This company offers floatplane tours in summer from Sitka with remote water landings. Phone (907) 747-8253 or (907) 752-0033.

Sitka Scenic Air Tours, 264 Katlian St., Sitka:

■ Scenic Air's flightseeing tours in a 25-mile radius of Sitka include Mount Edgecumbe and close-in parts of Baranof Island. Video tapes of the tour are available for an extra charge. Phone (907 747-6749.

Boat Tours

Prices range considerably, with guided water tours starting at about $80 per adult. The single listing here is the only non-charter boat company in Sitka running regular tours. For a full listing of charter boat operators offering wildlife viewing excursions, as well as sport fishing, contact the Sitka Convention and Visitors Bureau. Also see page 80 for more about boat and kayak tours and rentals.

Sea Otter & Wildlife Quest, Allen Marine Tours, P.O. Box 1049, Sitka:

■ High speed, 49-passenger boats depart three times a week in summer from Crescent Harbor for wildlife tours. The cruise to and from Salisbury Sound takes about 3.5 hours. Phone (907) 747-8100.

7 Beaver Lake Trail

(Length one way, .8 mile; hiking time one way, 40 minutes.) This trail, good for family outings, begins across the bridge at the Sawmill Creek Campground, 1.5 miles out the road to Blue Lake that branches off Sawmill Creek Road at the pulp mill. Switchbacks early on climb about 200 feet, then the trail levels out for an easy walk on planked boardwalk through muskeg and open forest. Bring your fishing pole because Beaver Lake has been stocked with grayling.

A hiker enjoys ridge walking above Sitka. (Dan Evans)

A road and two trails wind through Kruzof Island:

Kruzof Island Road

(Length one way 4.6 miles; hiking time one way, 2 to 3 hours.) Easy trail on old logging road from Mud Bay on island's east coast to Iris Meadows. Carry compass and map because vandalism has made the signs unreliable.

Mount Edgecumbe Trail

(Length one way 6.7 miles; hiking time one way, 4 to 6 hours.) Difficult trail from Fred's Creek cabin on island's east shore to summit crater. Trail, constructed by Civilian Conservation Corps in 1930s, can be wet. Final 3 miles are steep. Watch for bears. About 4 miles in on the trail, a spur leads to a three-sided shelter. Trail ends at 2,000 feet; to reach the summit, hike straight up. Remember that weather can diminish visibility and that there are no landmarks above tree line. If you use trail markers, please remove them when you leave.

Sealion Cove Trail

(Length one way, 2.5 miles; hiking time one way, 2 hours.)

This moderately difficult trail begins at the southern end of Kalinin Bay on the island's north end and continues to a mile-long white, sandy beach at Sealion Cove. Midway, the trail skirts a small lake good for swimming, although the water is very cold. ■

Sitka and the surrounding area sprawl below a trail on Mount Verstovia. (Dan Evans)

Sitka By Water

Sitka's other side, its ocean world, beckons with humpback whales, sea otters, sea lions, puffins, auklets, eagles and some of the best saltwater fishing in Southeast.

As an island town, Sitka has more shoreline than roads and encompasses almost as much water as land. Life naturally includes the sea. Sitkans fish for food, for income, for fun. Boats are more necessary than cars for many here, particularly fishermen and those who live on islands in the sound and commute to town by skiff. The ocean is never far from sight or sound, smell or touch, no matter what direction you go on land.

It's easy to experience Sitka's ocean world. Almost any place in town affords scenes of the sea, and getting out on the water is no problem either.

Several roads lead to oceanside parks with picnic tables and wildlife viewing platforms. Watch for humpbacks feeding along shore; October through May are the best months to see whales close to town. These humpbacks are found throughout summer in Southeast waters, but move closer to land as they feed on herring fish runs in late fall, early winter and early spring. Most of Southeast's humpbacks swim south sometime in winter to mate and calve in warmer waters, primarily the Hawaiian Islands. The newly completed Whale Park, off Sawmill Creek Road near the entrance to Silver Bay, has binocular-equipped gazebos for comfortable whale and sometimes, sea otter viewing.

The city's four public boat harbors allow for different marine encounters. Sitka's picturesque Crescent Harbor, located downtown near the Centennial Building visitor center and museum, bustles with boats. Stroll the docks to

This view shows a slice of Sitka's ocean world, Sitka Sound. (Ernest Manewal)

see deckhands at work, or take in the ambiance with a view of Mount Edgecumbe from the adjacent waterfront park. Explore the beach along Lincoln Street, just a short walk from downtown toward Sitka National Historical Park. Driftwood logs and rocky boulders make front row seats for basking in the glow of sunset across the sound.

Sitka Sound, with its numerous islands, stretches like a marine playground. Here you can stay overnight in an operational lighthouse complete with an outdoor hot tub, or book accommodations in a private island lodge, or fall asleep to the gentle ocean swells on a yacht, or watch the wildlife in a secluded bay from the dock of a floating guest house.

Fishing, birding, wildlife tours, photography, island hopping, volcanoes, scuba diving, even surfing for the experienced and adventurous await in Sitka's ocean world.

Boat Charters for Fishing, Wildlife Viewing

Dozens of charter companies offer boat tours and fishing excursions.

Boat charters targeting salmon and halibut start at $75 per person for a half-day and $140 per person full-day. Sport fishing licenses cost extra, starting at $10, and are sold at

several businesses in town and on board many of the charter
vessels.

Peak ocean fishing for king salmon is mid-May through
June, although they may bite on trolled or drifted herring
from mid-March through October. Silver salmon are available
June through September, although the best fishing for this
species is in August. Herring or large spoons are used for bait
with flashers for attraction. Halibut season goes late May
through early November, peaking in inside waters in late
August. Octopus and herring
are the preferred baits. Sitka's
halibut can be monsters,
exceeding 300 pounds.

*Humpback whales migrate past
Sitka. (Tom Soucek)*

Rockfish such as red snapper are caught year-round. Fishing derbies through the summer, with prizes to derby ticket holders for the largest fish, make fishermen careful about what big fish stories they tell.

Wildlife tours to see whales, otters, seals and sea lions along with water birds and land mammals, such as bears, are offered by numerous charter boat operators. Although Steller sea lions and harbor seal populations have plunged in their northern range, their numbers appear to be stable in Southeast, so a boat tour from Sitka is one way to perhaps see these increasingly threatened animals in the wild. Some charter boat operators specialize in wildlife and photography tours, and carry hydrophones to help locate whales under-water. The rates are similar to those charged by fishing charters. Some offer multiday touring packages.

The Mariner's Wall, at ANB Harbor on Katlian Street, honors the area's fishermen. The 40-foot-long wall, designed as a tribute by Southeast Alaska Women in Fisheries, was completed in fall 1988 and faced with 1,269 memorial red bricks engraved with the names of mariners who have died at sea.

Each operator has favorite places to show clients, but St. Lazaria, part of Alaska Maritime National Wildlife Refuge, with its millions of migrating seabirds, tops the wildlife viewing list for many.

Most of the fishing charter and tour boat operators require a two-passenger minimum and a six-person maximum, and will combine parties if needed.

Cruise ship passengers can make charter arrangements from on board. Several operators in Sitka cater to the cruise ships, offering a variety of trips.

Visitors arriving by ferry or airplane can schedule charters departing from Crescent and Thomsen harbors. The Sitka Convention and Visitors Bureau has up-to-date lists of charter operators and their services, and several are listed in the telephone yellow pages.

An alternative to chartering is offered by Allen Marine with its Sea Otter and Wildlife Quest tours on larger passenger boats. The company runs trips for cruise ship passengers, but also offers wildlife tours three times a week out of Crescent Harbor for independent travelers. A seat on

(continued on page 86)

Sitka's Harbors

If you're sailing to Sitka in your own boat, you need to contact the Sitka Harbormaster's Office on arrival to find a place to dock.

The office monitors VHF channel 16 and is physically located at Thomsen Harbor at the north end of the channel.

The city operates two transient moorage floats, one outside ANB Harbor, downtown near the east end of the bridge to Japonski Island; and another inside Thomsen Harbor. No reservations are accepted in advance; space is assigned on a first-come basis.

During the busiest weeks of summer, the harbors fill up with commercial fishermen, charter boat operators and visiting vessels. Boats may be rafted four and five deep at the transient floats during these

Colorful floats dangle from a Sitka fishing boat. (Harry M. Walker)

times. Sometimes things get so crowded that boats anchor in the sound or tie up to a floating breakwater until harbor space becomes available.

Boats in town for a prolonged visit can request a stall with or without electricity. The harbormaster puts visitors in stalls temporarily vacated by permanent users who are out of port.

Transient vessels are allowed in ANB Harbor, Sealing Cove Harbor on Japonski Island at the west end of the bridge, and at Thomsen Harbor. No transients may use Crescent Harbor downtown, although vessels carrying cruise ship passengers unload here at the city's lightering float.

ANB Harbor is Sitka's smallest, with only 87 stalls. People may live aboard their vessels in this harbor.

Thomsen Harbor holds about 275 boats, with an addition planned to take another 135. This expansion should slightly ease the demand for permanent moorage; the harbormaster has a waiting list of 500 vessels.

Sealing Cove Harbor and Crescent Harbor each hold about 400

ABOVE: *Fishing boats are tied up at ANB Harbor, Sitka's smallest. (Harry M. Walker)*

LEFT: *A sport fisherman weighs his silver salmon derby entry. (Ernest Manewal)*

boats. An RV park is adjacent to Sealing Cove Harbor.

The city charges 24 cents a foot per day to visiting boats for dock space; the cost doubles if the owner asks to be billed by mail. Monthly and seasonal permits are available to transient vessels at a lower charge. Electrical hook-ups cost extra.

Fresh water and restrooms are located at each of Sitka's public harbors. An array of marine services and supplies—such as fuels, electrical repairs, hull and fiberglass work, and welding—are available from businesses in town.

Steller sea lions, a threatened species on decline in most of the North Pacific, are still healthy in Southeast. (Dan Evans)

one of its 50-passenger jet boats to Salisbury Sound, a 3.5-hour cruise 25 miles north of Sitka, costs $80 for adults and less for children. The company guarantees you'll see wildlife, or it promises to refund part of your fare.

Families and groups seeking a sailing vacation of their own design can check out several operators offering extended yacht cruises out of Sitka through the passages and secluded inlets of this Pacific coastline. Figure on spending $200 to $500 a night per person for a berth on a private sailboat or yacht. Many of these cruises deliver special touches, from gourmet meals to personal wildlife guides.

Caren and John Yerkes started offering pleasure cruises as Sitka Sportfishing Charters several years ago, turning their interests in boating, fishing and sightseeing into a way for their eldest son, Josh, to earn money for college. Josh and father John are both licensed captains, taking small groups and families out on their 38-foot yacht *Rubato*, for overnight or weeklong cruises through the islands.

Boating is a way of life for the Yerkes, who live on a small island in the sound and commute to winter jobs in town by skiff. "It takes a little more planning to live on an island," says Caren. Even so, they have city electricity and their house is plumbed to use drinking water produced from a desalinator. They also collect rain water for washing.

Sea Kayaking

Numerous bays, sheltered water passages, and miles of wilderness shoreline make Sitka one of the premiere kayaking locations in Alaska.

Guided kayak trips starting at about $70 for adults, less

for children, are available from at least two companies, Alaska Travel Adventures and Sitka Sound Ocean Adventures. Sitka Sound also rents skiffs starting at $60 a day.

Or you can rent kayaks and go off on your own. Baidarka

Mount Edgecumbe Volcano

Sixteen miles west of Sitka, Mount Edgecumbe volcano dominates the horizon. This 3,201-foot mountain, with its snow-frosted truncated cone, compares in appearance to Japan's Mount Fuji.

Mount Edgecumbe and neighboring vents on southern Kruzof Island have not erupted in historic times. The vents were, however, the source of numerous major ash eruptions 10,000 to 12,000 years ago; the ash deposits are nearly three feet thick in Sitka and can be found as far north as Yakutat, Glacier Bay and Juneau. The latest known eruptions on Kruzof Island, from a vent near Mount Edgecumbe, produced two small ash deposits between 4,000 and 5,000 years ago.

Mount Edgecumbe's cone and the adjacent domes of Crater Ridge are the most visible volcanic features on southern Kruzof Island. These features, together with six smaller cones, make up a volcanic field on Kruzof that became active 600,000 years ago, during the Pleistocene epoch. Although there are small lava flows elsewhere in the region and seamounts in the Gulf of Alaska are actually submarine volcanoes, the Mount Edgecumbe volcanic field is unusual in Southeast for the volume of its eruptive deposits. The field is also notable for its proximity to the offshore Fairweather fault, the geological boundary between the Pacific and North American plates. Scientists are unsure exactly why Mount Edgecumbe formed, but it seems to be the result of northward movement of the Pacific plate past Kruzof Island.

While Mount Edgecumbe is officially classified as dormant, humans added spice to the volcano's history in April 1974 when a group dubbed the "Dirty Dozen" chartered a helicopter from Petersburg, southeast of Sitka, to carry 70 old tires into the volcano's cone. They set fire to the tires, then waited for reports of a volcanic eruption to reach Sitka. Sure enough, the reports came. Those who investigated the eruption found "April Fool" stamped in the snow beside the tires. The charred tires remain in the crater to this day.

A new field guide to Mount Edgecumbe, containing its geologic history and information about hiking to the volcano's summit, is due out sometime in 1996, a joint project of the U.S. Forest Service and the U.S. Geological Survey. To obtain a copy, contact the Sitka Ranger District, 201 Katlian, Suite 109, Sitka.

A boater watches the sunrise from his bidarka. (Dan Evans)

Boats, downtown on Lincoln Street, upstairs from Old Harbor Books, has been in business since 1977. Owner Larry Edwards has been paddling the area even longer. He also offers custom guided sea kayaking trips, but most of his rental business is with people planning their own trips. Single and double kayaks with a full complement of paddling gear – life jackets, flares, sea socks, bilge pumps, sponges – are available starting at $25 a half-day. He also provides maps of the area, with advice on what's private land and what's not.

He requires clients to demonstrate proficiency or take a kayak safety short-course, offered at the harbor for $25 per group. You need to bring rain gear and wear old sneakers, Teva sandals or rubber boots that can get wet. You also need to provide food, water bottles and camping gear for extended trips.

Baidarka Boats also rents folding kayaks, good for stowing aboard floatplanes or taxi boats for drop-offs at remote paddling locations, such as the South Baranof Wilderness or West Chichagof-Yakobi Wilderness. (See page 96 for information about these areas.)

Seaside Cabins

Another way to enjoy Sitka's ocean world is by staying in a remote seaside cabin. The upscale version of ocean hideaways includes those offered by Sitka-area wilderness and fishing lodges and private inns. An alternative are the 11 oceanfront public use cabins, available at $25 a night from the U.S. Forest Service. These do require boat or floatplane drop-offs and pick-ups.

Contact the Sitka Ranger District, 201 Katlian, Suite 109, Sitka, phone (907) 747 6671, for detailed information about the cabins and to schedule their use. The cabins can be reserved as much as 180 days in advance, and some of them book up quickly. Two of the most popular are cabins close in, at Samsing Cove, 5.5 miles south of town, and at Allan Point, 16 miles north.

Other popular Forest Service cabins include those on Kruzof Island: an A-frame at Fred's Creek, 10 miles west of Sitka at the Mount Edgecumbe trailhead, and the Shelikof Bay cabin on the outer coast of Kruzof, with trails leading to Iris Meadows and Mud Bay.

Arriving By Boat

If you plan to sail a boat around Sitka Sound and need nautical charts, they are available from Old Harbor Books on Lincoln Street and Murray Pacific Supply Corp. on Katlian Street.

(continued on page 92)

St. Lazaria

About 15 miles by boat southwest of Sitka, the 65-acre, volcanic island of St. Lazaria rises in Sitka Sound. The island, a wildlife refuge since 1909, was designated a wilderness area in October 1970 and incorporated into the Alaska Maritime National Wildlife Refuge in 1980.

St. Lazaria's claim to refuge status stems from its important seabird colonies, sheltering half a million birds of 10 species. Tufted puffins, rhinoceros auklets, ancient murrelets, and, most abundant, fork-tailed and Leach's storm-petrels burrow into the volcanic soils. Glaucous-winged gulls nest in clumps of vegetation.

LEFT: *Sea urchins abound in waters near Sitka. (Ernest Manewal)*

BELOW: *Visitors to St. Lazaria Island refuge are treated to spectacular views of Mount Edgecumbe. (Ernest Manewal)*

Common and thick-billed murres, pelagic cormorants and pigeon guillemots lay their eggs on rocky sea cliffs. Horned puffins used to nest on the island but have not been reported nesting there in recent years.

The island's thick vegetation, a tangle of salmonberry and elderberry in the center with stands of Sitka spruce at the east and west ends, all encircled by a fringe of cow parsnip, hide song and fox sparrows, hermit and Swainson's thrushes, orange-crowned warblers, winter wrens and rufous hummingbirds.

Several other species are often visible from boats offshore: red-faced cormorants; herring and mew gulls; black-legged kittiwakes; Cassin's auklets, marbled and Kittlitz's murrelets; black oyster-catchers, a shorebird that breeds on the island; peregrine falcons and, of course, bald eagles. Seasonal migrants to the island include great blue heron, spotted sandpiper, whimbrel, belted kingfisher and green-winged teal. Brown bear and Sitka black-tailed deer occasionally swim over from Kruzof Island, 1.5 miles to the north, and land otters visit St. Lazaria at times to prey on seabird eggs. Steller sea lions, sea otters and harbor seals swim in nearby waters, although the drastic decline in sea lion and harbor seal populations in recent years makes their sighting less likely.

St. Lazaria, named in 1809 by Russian navigator Ivan Vasiliev, is uninhabited, and except for a period during World War II when it was the site of fire control stations and a coastal radar position for surface craft, the island appears to have been uninhabited since prehistoric times. Thick vegetation has obscured most signs of the World War II camps. This same vegetation and the rugged terrain

discourage hiking. Intruders can crush the burrows of ground-nesting birds and frighten parents from cliff-side nests.

In favorable weather, St. Lazaria is a 45-minute trip one-way in a six-passenger boat. There are no easy landing sites for small boats (commercial tour operators must have a permit to land), and visitors can best appreciate the island from offshore.

Tufted puffins nest at St. Lazaria Island. (Dan Evans)

ABOVE: *A sailboat plies the waters of Sitka Sound. (Harry M. Walker)*

LEFT: *Beachcombers find glass floats near Sitka. (Dan Evans)*

Alaska Marine Highway ferries serve Sitka regularly from Ketchikan and Juneau, and the town is a regular port-of-call for most all the cruise ships sailing the Inside Passage.

Recreational mariners and commercial fishermen boating into Sitka need to first check in with the Sitka harbormaster for moorage availability and listing of various services. Boat slips are at a premium here, and transient moorage may be found at three of the four Sitka harbors.

Way Out and Down

The underside of Sitka's ocean world beckons with beautiful diving, a secret that's not so secret anymore. For the past couple of decades, a core of resident scuba divers

Sitka diver Bill Coltharp surfaces with king crab (Dan Evans)

have explored Sitka's underwater sights almost by themselves, but now more and more divers from far off are taking a plunge while they're in town.

Octopus, wolf eels (so ugly they're cute), rockfish, halibut, salmon, needlefish, jelly fish, sea pins, sea fans, sponges and more than 25 varieties of starfish are some of the creatures inhabiting the depths.

Many of Sitka's local divers learned the sport when commercial sea cucumber and abalone fisheries started up in the early 1980s, the harvests going to mainly Asian markets. The fisheries still go on each winter, although the divers have to travel farther from town now to find harvestable quantities. It's not a big money fishery, but the divers usually make enough to pay for their gear so they can keep diving.

At the same time, the sport seems to be growing in popularity. The local dive shop sees more than 80 visiting scuba divers each summer. It seems a favorite sport with cruise ship crews, says Tim White, manager of Southeast Diving and Sports on Lincoln Street.

The shop rents the full scuba set-up, $60 a day, to certified open water divers. Dry-suits are recommended – even in summer, temperatures at diving depths are only in the high 40s; dry-suit certification can be obtained in a one-day course for $150. Diving is best August through March, when water visibility often exceeds 100 feet. The water clouds up in summer, and visibility drops to 15 or 20 feet.

Good diving areas abound, except for a few places with dangerous currents. Maps and advice are available from the folks at the dive shop, and they can arrange trips with the local charter companies that operate boats set up for diving.

Snorkeling also attracts people in summer, when low tide brings sights of abalone and Dungeness crab. Summer water temperatures at the surface warm up to about 60 degrees,

Sport Fishing

Alaska Department of Fish and Game publishes a 16-page free guide to sport fishing in Sitka, complete with maps. The guide is available at various locations around town or you can stop in the Alaska Department of Fish and Game office, 304 Lake Street, Room 103. Phone (907) 747-5355. You can write for a copy in advance. The agency offers a comparable publication for sport hunting.

The U.S. Forest Service also publishes free guides to recreational fishing/wildlife opportunities at public use cabins in the Sitka area. These are available from the Sitka Ranger District, 201 Katlian Street, Suite 109. Phone (907) 747-6671.

A sample of local fishing with the species of fish and type of access includes:

Beaver Lake:	Arctic grayling. Trail.
Blue Lake:	Rainbow trout. Road.
Green Lake Reservoir:	Brook trout. Bike and foot.
Heart Lake:	Brook trout. Trail.
Indian River:	Dolly Varden. Trail and road.
Starrigavan Creek:	Rainbow trout, steelhead. Road.
Swan Lake:	Variety of trout. Road, foot, bicycle.
Thimbleberry Lake:	Brook trout. Trail.

There are two salmon hatcheries in the Sitka area. The Northern Southeast Regional Aquaculture Association operates a hatchery in town. Sheldon Jackson College has a small hatchery for its fisheries technology students. Neither hatchery is open to the public.

so wet suits usually provide adequate insulation and are preferred for snorkeling over the more bulky dry suits.

You might also notice the cars and trucks driving around Sitka toting surf boards. Surfing may seem an obscure water sport for the north, but Sitka has gained fame among the world's surfing elite as one of the more exotic locales to ride a break.

It's unclear how many surfers actually live in Sitka, but there are at least a few. *Surfer Magazine* even came to town a couple of years ago to check it out. Surfing is best in winter, say those who know, when the big breakers roll in off the stormy Pacific. Shelikof Bay and Sea Lion Cove on the outer coast of Kruzof Island and Shoals Point on the island's southeastern tip are the surfing hot spots, along with Sandy Beach outside town off Halibut Point Road. Even if you don't want to hang ten, these northern surfers may be worth watching. ■

Area waters teem with colorful sea stars. (Dan Evans)

The Wild Yonder

Sitka is a jumping off place for two U.S. Forest Service Wilderness areas within Tongass National Forest.

■ **South Baranof Wilderness** cuts a swath across the upper half of southern Baranof Island. The coastline is deeply indented with bays and inlets set against the towering backdrop of steep mountains. The highest point in the Wilderness is glaciated Mount Ada, at 4,528 feet.

Permanent snowfields and glaciers cover much of the upper elevations above timberline, which starts at about 2,000 feet. Waterfalls cascade down the mountains near the coast. Glaciers extended to the coast during the last ice age and left u-shaped valleys when they receded.

This 319,568-acre Wilderness is home to Sitka black-tailed deer, brown bear, mink, marten and land otter, as well as bald eagles, song- and waterbirds. The Wilderness holds many of the island's major steelhead-producing lakes.

Parts of the Wilderness are some of the rainiest areas in Southeast. More than 200 inches of precipitation are recorded annually at a weather station on the island's east coast, at Little Port Walter just outside the Wilderness boundary.

The Wilderness' lower west side, exposed to the Pacific Ocean, can experience violent storms with winds exceeding 100 mph. Smaller offshore islands buffer the upper western coast adjacent to Sitka Sound, offering more protected waterways and fiords attractive to kayakers and other recreational boaters.

Three Forest Service recreation cabins are located in the Wilderness at Avoss Lake, Davidof Lake and Plotnikof Lake.

Old gold mining camps along Chicagof Island's coast include this one on Slocum Arm. (Dan Evans)

All can be reached by floatplane from Sitka, and rowing skiffs are provided at each location.

Avoss Lake, high in the alpine country about 30 miles southeast of Sitka, has Dolly Varden and rainbow trout. The cabin bunks six to eight people. Davidof and Plotnikof are both mountain lakes, about 40 miles out from Sitka. They are connected by trail, although maintenance is infrequent. From south to north, the trail begins behind the Plotnikof Lake cabin and ends at the south side of Davidof Lake. The cabin at Davidof bunks eight to 10. Both lakes have coho salmon, and Plotnikof has steelhead.

The cabins rent for $25 a night; reservations must be made through the Sitka Ranger District office, 201 Katlian, Suite 109, Sitka, phone (907) 747-6671.

■ **West Chichagof-Yakobi Wilderness** stretches along the western coastline of Chichagof and Yakobi islands, north from Sitka.

This 264,747-acre Wilderness is noted for its intricate coastline – small offshore islands, reefs and promontories, protected bays, coves, lagoons and passages, tidal meadows and estuaries. About a third of the Wilderness is old-growth forest of western hemlock and Sitka spruce. The uplands are sculpted by numerous snow- and ice-covered peaks.

The Wilderness extends from Cross Sound on the north to Salisbury Sound on the south. The community of Pelican is

The alpine Rosenberg Ridge rises above Nakwasina Sound, north of Sitka on Baranof Island. (Dan Evans)

Backcountry travelers can fly to public use cabins in areas like this, at Baranof Lake east of Sitka. (Ernest Manewal)

just outside the wilderness' eastern boundary on Lisianski Inlet, Chichagof Island. The Tlingit community of Hoonah is about 35 miles east of the Wilderness and Sitka is located 20 miles south.

Sitka black-tailed deer and brown bear share the Wilderness, along with remarkable populations of migrant waterfowl and marine mammals. Rafts of sea otters are commonly seen among the islands and in the offshore kelp patches. Humpback whales can often be seen offshore, and a population of gray whales frequent the Bertha Bay area. Harbor seals live along most of the coastline and large Steller sea lion rookeries are located at White Sister Islands, Cape Cross and Cape Bingham.

Part of the area's history includes mining. Gold discovered by a Native fisherman in 1905, in a stream at the head of Klag Bay on Chichagof Island's west coast, sparked a small stampede and settlement of Chichagof mining town. The Chichagof Mine and the Hirst-Chichagof Mine, which opened about 1922 on nearby Kimshan Cove, were major gold producers and yielded small amounts of silver. Largely because of these mines, the Sitka area grew to be an important contributor to gold production in Southeast; mines on southwestern Chichagof Island were second only to mines near Juneau in total lode-gold production until gold mining was suspended during World War II.

Today the privately owned Chichagof and Hirst-Chichagof mine properties are surrounded by the Wilderness. Other old mining prospects now part of the Wilderness include a small gold and copper mine near Goulding Harbor that was linked to water by a 5-mile-long railroad built in the 1920s; an old

Hot springs are popular destinations on Chicagof and Baranof islands. (Dan Evans)

engine and some pieces of track in the weeds are evidence of that venture.

One way to experience the West Chichagof-Yakobi Wilderness is by kayak. A nice trip includes paddling nearly the entire Wilderness coastline in one direction between Sitka and Pelican, riding the state ferry for the other leg of the trip. This trip includes some open crossings, so allow time for possible weather delays.

Four Forest Service recreation cabins are located in this Wilderness. The Sitka Ranger District handles reservations for three cabins on the west coast of Chichagof Island, at Goulding Lake, White Sulphur Hot Springs and Suloia Lake. A cabin in Greentop Harbor on Yakobi Island may be booked through the Hoonah Ranger District, P.O. Box 135, Hoonah 99829, phone (907) 945-3631.

Goulding and Suloia are both mountain lakes with floatplane access. The seaside cabin at White Sulphur Springs is one of the most popular. Only the cabin can be reserved; the bathhouse is open to any visitor and is frequently used by commercial fishermen, kayakers and campers. ■

Plants and Animals

Forests of western hemlock and Sitka spruce dominate Sitka area vegetation. Western hemlock can be recognized by its flat, round-tipped needles and distinctive droopy top. Sitka spruce has stiff, sharp-tipped needles, and an upright tree top (see page 104 for more on Sitka spruce). Other common trees include mountain hemlock, yellow cedar and red alder. The forest understory consists of rusty Menziesia, huckleberry, blueberry and devil's club. At the edges of forests and in clearings grow dense thickets of other shrubs such as salmonberry, crabapple and Sitka alder.

The forest floor is a moss-covered, decaying jumble of fallen trees. In some places, where adequate light is available, this floor itself may be a tiny forest of oak fern, bunchberry and single delight. In very dense forests where few plants can live, the forest floor appears to be almost lifeless.

Much of the land is covered by muskegs, or peat bogs, which range in size

Muskegs, or peat bogs, cover much of the area around Sitka. (Ernest Manewal)

from a few square feet to many acres. Sphagnum moss forms a spongy carpet of vegetation in these wet, essentially treeless areas. The hummocky carpet of low vegetation is broken by occasional pools and a few stunted lodgepole pines.

Old-growth hemlock soars at timberline. (Dan Evans)

Low-growing evergreen shrubs, numerous wildflowers and insect-eating plants are abundant in peat bogs. Bog-lovers will delight in bogs near Starrigavan Campground, along the Indian River Trail, up Harbor Mountain Road and along the Beaver Lake Trail.

During late spring and early summer, the upper beach meadows sparkle with red and yellow paintbrush, western columbine, yarrow, wild geranium, shooting star, buttercup, chocolate lily and cinquefoil. The Starrigavan Recreation Area highlights striking examples of beach meadows.

Above treeline, a mosaic of plant communities blanket the subalpine meadows and alpine tundra. These communities include lush meadows, heaths and windswept

Salmonberries, raspberries and blueberries thrive in the region's dense forest understory. (Ernest Manewal)

Black oystercatchers, with their distinctive bull's-eye eyes and bright red bill, are common Sitka area shorebirds. (Ernest Manewal)

rock outcrops. Plants are small and slow-growing. Lichens, heathers, clubmosses, sedges, grasses and stunted conifers abound. An array of flowers enliven the summer, and vivid autumn colors announce the approach of winter. The high country is frequently swept with the grays of clouds and rain. The juxtaposition of brightly colored flowers and foliage against the soft gray is unforgettable.

Just as the vegetation of Sitka creates memorable images, so too does the wildlife, from the whales that course through Sitka Sound, to the seabirds that thrive on precipitous, seaside cliffs, to the brown bears that stalk the forests to the mice, voles and bats that carry on their high-energy, low-visibility lifestyle under the noses of more

Sitka Spruce

Trees — lots of them — dominate first impressions of any visitor to Sitka. Among these evergreens is Alaska's state tree, the Sitka spruce.

One of seven spruce species native to the United States, the Sitka spruce (*Picea sitchensis*) was originally collected by Carl Mertens in June and July 1827. Mertens' samples were carried to St. Petersburg, Russia, where they were shown to August H.G. Bongard, a professor of botany. The professor gave the species its name, presumably because the collection presented to him was all from the Sitka area.

All of the world's spruce species inhabit cool, temperate climates of the Northern Hemisphere. Sitka spruce can live 750 years and can reach 225 feet high with trunks more than 10 feet in diameter. More common specimens grow 100 feet to 160 feet with trunks 3 feet to 5 feet in diameter. This species makes up about one-quarter of the Southeast Alaska forest, much of which lies within the spectacular 17-million-acre Tongass National Forest.

Quite strong in relation to its weight, the wood of Sitka spruce was used for aircraft construction during the first and second world wars. Today the wood is fashioned into piano and guitar sounding boards, gliders and boats, and is widely used in the construction industry.

To identify Sitka spruce on your walks around town, look for stiff, sharp needles that extend out on all sides of the twig. Note the thin bark, gray and smooth, that evolves into a purplish-brown with scaly plates on older growth. The cylindrical cones are usually 2 1/2 inches to 3 1/2 inches long.

The sea otter 's dense coat attracted Russian fur hunters to Sitka. (Ernest Manewal)

noticeable species. The town has given its name to one species of small mammal, the Sitka mouse, a subrace of the deer mouse.

Humpback and killer whales, sea lions, harbor seals and sea otters patrol Sitka marine waters; fresh waters support salmon, steelhead, cutthroat and rainbow trout and Dolly Varden. Marine waters abound in halibut, other finfish and a variety of shellfish. Land otters and mink feed on fish and small mammals that live in surrounding forests. Delicate Sitka black-tailed deer step daintily through a forest devoid of wolves, but must share their habitat with the powerful brown bears that inhabit Baranof, Chichagof and Admiralty islands.

Mountain goats, beavers, martens and red squirrels, while not native to the area, have been introduced to Baranof Island. Mountain goats have adapted well to their new environment and in 1995 were at an all-time high. Away from town in watersheds where trapping is prohibited, beavers too have flourished in their new habitat.

Many wildlife species find the area a perfect home, and their presence adds immeasurably to any visit to Sitka. ∎

Calendar of Events

■ **January:**
Russian Christmas and Starring (Jan. 7)
Northwest Coast Arts Symposium (mid-month: for 1996,
Jan. 15-26)
Interline Classic Basketball Tournament (3rd week; for
1996, Jan. 17-20)
Whale Watching, as humpbacks feed near Sitka (entire
month)

■ **February:**
Read a good book.

■ **March:**
Herring fishery: Wildlife is generally abundant as herring
gather and spawn in Sitka waters.

■ **April:**
Herring fishery.

■ **May:**
Mayfest (entire month)
Mother's Day Quilt Show (for 1996, May 6-17)
Annual Julie Hughes Triathlon (3rd Saturday; for 1996,
May 18)
Sitka Salmon Derby (last weekend; for 1996, May 25-27)

■ **June:**
Sitka Salmon Derby (first weekend; for 1996, June 1-3)
Sitka Summer Music Festival (starts first Friday; for 1996,
June 7, 11, 14, 18, 21, 25, 28.)

Island Institute humanities/writer's symposium (mid-June; 1996 dates TBA)

▪ July:

July 4th Celebration (July 2-4)
10K Run (on a Saturday near the 4th; 1996 dates TBA)

Fourth of July celebrations include a swimming race in Crescent Harbor. (Ernest Manewal)

A costumed Keystone Kop celebrates Alaska Day. (Ernest Manewal)

Bike Races (early July; 1996 dates TBA)
Gavan Hill Mountain Run (late July; 1996 date TBA)

◾ August:
Halibut Derby (2nd weekend in August; for 1996, Aug. 10-11)
Soggy Trot half-marathon (1996 date TBA)
Hank LeClerc Memorial Mountain Run (1996 date TBA)

◾ September:
Mudball Classic Softball Tournament (Labor Day Weekend)

◾ October:
Alaska Day Festival (Oct. 14-18)
Alaska Day Race (1996 date TBA)
Mountain Madness bicycle race (mid-month; for 1996, Oct. 20)
Whale Watching, as humpbacks feed near Sitka (entire month)

◾ November:
Turkey Trot Fun Run and Walk (Thanksgiving Day morning)
Holiday Fest of concerts, bazaars, fashion shows, extended shopping hours (entire month)
Whale Watching (entire month)

◾ December:
Holiday Fest (entire month)
Whale Watching (entire month)

Summer Fine Arts in Sitka

Special things happen in Sitka, especially during June.

■ **The Sitka Summer Music Festival** brings three weeks of classical chamber music to town, with the opening concert of the series held the first Friday in June. The festival celebrates its 25th anniversary in 1996.

Concerts on Friday and Tuesday nights begin at 8:15 in the Centennial Building auditorium. Those interested in learning about the selections to be performed and their composers can attend brief preconcert lectures, or "informances," starting at 7:30 p.m.

Due to the number of season tickets sold each year, advance single concert tickets are limited. It's advisable to purchase tickets early by writing the festival office at P.O. Box 3333, Sitka; or by calling (907) 27SITKA until May 15 or (907) 747-6774 after May 15. Prices are $12 for adults; $6 for youths ages 6 to 18 and senior citizens.

Violinist Paul Rosenthal initiated the festival after he visited Sitka in 1971. He was so inspired by the surroundings that he decided to hold an informal reunion here with fellow protégés from the Jascha Heifetz and Gregor Piatigorsky master classes. A handful of people contributed enough money to buy the musicians one-way tickets to Sitka, and enough people attended the concerts to pay their way back home. The musicians performed without fee and have volunteered their talents every year since.

Today, more than 20 acclaimed musicians gather in Sitka to play during the festival. "Perhaps it is because in Sitka we don't play for money or glory that the music itself and the concerts mean so much to us," founder Rosenthal has said.

Classical musicians play chamber music in view of Sitka Sound. (Courtesy of Sitka Summer Music Festival)

"Whatever the reason – and I believe it is better not to look too closely into such mysteries – a very large percentage of the performances at the Sitka festival have that extra something that makes all of us, performers and audience alike, feel the special joy that is the gift of great music, lovingly played and heard."

■ Occurring simultaneously during the music festival is the **Symposium on Human Values and the Written Word**, formerly known as the Sitka Summer Writer's Symposium.

The symposium is the core program of The Island Institute, a non-profit organization based in Sitka that fosters discussions on social and cultural issues, bringing together viewpoints from humanities, arts and sciences. In addition to the symposium, at other times in the year the institute sponsors a Resident Fellows program for visual artists, writers and humanities scholars; community forums about local issues; and a Visiting Writers Series to bring recognized poets, novelists and short story authors to Sitka.

The week-long Symposium on Human Values and the Written Word is led by a faculty of recognized writers and thinkers, including poets and astronomers, anthropologists and novelists, natural historians, philosophers, linguists and folklorists. Past faculty writers have included Barry Lopez, Margaret Atwood and Terry Tempest Williams.

Readings by symposium faculty in the evenings are open to the public and single tickets are available for various lectures. Registration for the symposium is limited to 55 participants at a cost of $220 for registration before May 1, and $250 after that date. Housing on the Sheldon Jackson College campus is available for an additional fee. For more information about the symposium or other institute programs, write The Island Institute, P.O. Box 2420, Sitka, or call (907) 747-3794.

■ A third cultural happening in June is the **Sitka Fine Arts Camp** for youth.

The camp, sponsored by the non-profit Alaska Arts Southeast, offers classes in a spectrum of fine arts disciplines for students grades 6 through 12. Most of the 84 youngsters attending the camp in 1995 were from Southeast, although some came from as far away as Interior Alaska and Oregon. The faculty of professional artists, many from outside Alaska, offer instruction in musical theater, jazz band and vocals, modern dance, scene work, paper making, watercolors, drawing, mime, computer graphics, computers and music, and printmaking, among others.

Faculty presentations are open to the public during the opening of camp, and students show their work during two days of visual arts displays and stage performances at the end of camp.

The Sitka Fine Arts Camp is usually held during the last part of June at Mount Edgecumbe High School and the adjacent University of Alaska campus. Tuition for full-time attendance ranges from $500 to $600 with housing. Part-time registration is also available. For more information, write The Sitka Fine Arts Camp at 114B Harvest Way, Sitka, or call (907) 747 7860. ■

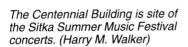

The Centennial Building is site of the Sitka Summer Music Festival concerts. (Harry M. Walker)

Children's Favorites

On the Sitka sightseeing circuit, children will enjoy:

■ **The Alaska Raptor Rehabilitation Center** is a hit with children of all ages. Along with owls and eagles to see, there are feathers, talons, bones and wings to feel. There's an adopt-a-raptor program, and a gift shop with books and raptor things. Kids may want to see the center's rodent colony as well; it's not part of the regular tour but is shown on request...and this happens often.

■ **The Sitka National Historical Park** offers summer children's programs ranging from storytelling to nature walks. Check schedules posted weekly at the park's visitor center, around town and published in the newspaper. This is a great place for kids anytime, with the beach to comb for shells, starfish and other sea life, and forest trails and the totem park to explore, in addition to the center's exhibits.

■ Numerous **charter boat and tour operators** offer discounted tickets for children; be sure to ask when you're booking. One of these, Outercoast Charters, (907) 747 8114, specializes in family fishing charters with kids under 10 free and ages 10 to 14 at half-price. Families with older children may want to check into kayak or skiff rentals for guided or self-guided trips.

Around town, amusements for children include:

■ **Sandy Beach**, a public beach on Halibut Point Road about two miles from downtown, draws swimmers and sunbathers, probably because of its expanse of sandy beach during low tide. There's no lifeguard on duty here, or anywhere else along shore, but you're likely to see children swimming during summer regardless of how cold it seems.

Logan Evans takes a break from a rain forest outing. (Dan Evans)

■ For warmer splashing, two **indoor pools** offer public hours. The pool at Blatchley Middle School, 601 Halibut Point Road, is open evenings. Flotation devices are available for youngsters. Call the pool at (907) 747-5677 or Community Schools at (907) 747-8670 for hours.

On the Sheldon Jackson College campus, the pool at Hames P.E. Center, 801 Lincoln, is open various times through the week. Call the center, (907) 747-5231, for hours.

■ Young children clamoring for climbers and slides will particularly like the Verstovia Elementary School **playground**, 307 Kashevaroff. There's even a basketball court under cover, a nice touch for this rain forest town to keep the hoopsters happy.

■ **The Kettleson Memorial Library** conducts a summer reading program for children, with games and prizes. During the school year, the library holds a preschool story hour, generally on Tuesday mornings.

■ **The Coliseum Twin Theatre**, 315 Lincoln, shows first run movies, sometimes family fare, on the weekends.

■ **The Sitka Bowling Center**, 331 Lincoln, is open year-round. One lane is reserved especially for children, with gutter bumpers to keep the ball in the alley. Summertime specials, $1 to $1.50 a game with $1 shoe rentals, make this relatively cheap entertainment. The place stays busy fall through winter, when most of the lanes are tied up at night with leagues.

■ Sitka's **bike paths, bike lanes and trails** make it possible to pedal along the coast and through the rain forest from one end of town practically to the other. (See page 62 for information on bike rentals). Take along a fishing pole, with the proper permits of course, and dip a line at any number of holes along the way to spend a day doing what the locals do.

Exploring Sitka's shore includes looking for abalone. (Dan Evans)

■ **Hiking** always holds promise for an enjoyable family outing, particularly if you choose a route within the abilities of your group. See page 72 for a description of Sitka's most popular trails.

■ Sitka is dotted with **picnic areas**. Among them: the forested, beachfront Halibut Point picnic area, with covered shelters along the sea for views of Sitka Sound, 2.5 miles north of town on Halibut Point Road; the Harbor Mountain picnic area open in summer, at the top of the five-mile gravel road up the mountain; and the state's Pioneer Park picnic area on Halibut Point Road just past the Sea Mart grocery.

■ **Whale Park**, about six miles from town on Sawmill Creek Road, is a beauty of a little park with a fantastic view of Silver Bay. It's a good place to take kids to watch humpback whales feeding close to town, since the gazebos have binoculars to use. The kids will also like climbing on the big, concrete sculpture of breaching whales located near the picnic area. There's even a full-size whale painted on the surface of the parking lot, so kids can do a little body-size comparisons. One of the three boardwalks is wheelchair accessible, as is one of the gazebos. The other two boardwalks lead down to the beach. Interpretive signs telling about whales, other wildlife and plants in the area help the kids learn about what they're seeing.

■ **The Starrigavan Recreation Area** at the end of Halibut Point Road holds activities for kids of all ages. Located just a short walk from the parking lot is a bird-viewing platform that faces Starrigavan Bay. From here, you can see shorebirds wading in the shallows, ducks and geese feeding in the estuary, and songbirds and raptors overhead. The Estuary Life Trail, a quarter-mile-long fully accessible boardwalk, leads along the bay through saltwater grasses, alders and conifers to the river-viewing deck, which juts over Starrigavan Creek. Spawning salmon swarm here in late summer. Just past the river-viewing deck is the Forest and Muskeg Trail, which goes 3/4 mile through hemlock and Sitka spruce trees and a peat bog. The trail has interpretative signs and is barrier free, although the grade and distance may limit some visitors. Two other trails are planned for the recreation area: one will lead from the campground and picnic area around the edge of Mosquito Cove; the other will parallel the highway from the ferry terminal past Old Sitka State Historical Site to the recreation area parking lot. ■

Looking For A Place To Stay?

Sitka has more than 200 rooms in five hotels and motels, at least 20 bed and breakfasts, and numerous other privately operated rental accommodations, from vacation cottages and apartments to floating cabins and a lighthouse.

Here's a brief guide to some of Sitka's lodgings; for a more comprehensive list, particularly of bed and breakfasts, consult the Sitka Convention and Visitors Bureau or the Sitka yellow pages. It's wise to reserve rooms well in advance for summer visits.

Major credit cards are accepted by most; at least one place noted here gives a 4 percent discount to guests paying with cash. Some lodgings operate courtesy shuttles around town; otherwise visitors without cars can arrange for taxi service, or contact Sitka Tours for shuttle bus transportation, at a nominal fee, between their lodging and the airport, ferry terminal, or downtown. Several places listed here run fishing or sightseeing charters as well; others may help arrange charters with independent operators.

KEY TO PRICING*

$ — Inexpensive, $7 to $59 per night
$$ — Moderate, $60 to $125 per night
$$$ — Expensive, more than $125 per night

* Prices do not include Sitka's 4 percent bed tax and 4 percent sales tax. Summer rates are given; most establishments offer lower winter rates, from about mid-September to mid-May.

HOTELS/MOTELS

■ **Westmark Shee Atika, 330 Seward Street**

Located close to the waterfront and within easy walking distance of historic sites, the Shee Atika is Sitka's largest, nicest and spendiest hotel. It has 100 rooms, including three suites with excellent vistas of Sitka Sound overlooking Crescent Harbor; singles and doubles with ocean views are also available. This full-service hotel is a good choice if you like comfort, convenience, room-service and an on-site restaurant and bar. A visitor information kiosk operated by Sitka Tours is located in the lobby. The hotel also offers Alaska Airlines frequent flier miles. (907) 747-6241; fax (907) 747-5486. **$$$**

■ **Cascade Inn, 2035 Halibut Point Road**

This small inn, located about 2.5 miles from downtown, has 10 rooms, each with a private balcony overlooking the water. Non-smoking rooms and kitchenette units are available. A small convenience plaza with grocery, liquor store and video rental is located on premises. The inn also operates fishing charters, which guests may book for an extra charge. (800) 532-0908; (907) 747-6804; or fax (907) 747-6572. **$$**

■ **Potlatch Motel, 713 Katlian Street**

This 32-room motel is about six blocks from downtown. Some units have kitchenettes; non-smoking rooms are available. The motel operates a courtesy van to the airport, ferry terminal and downtown. A walk-in freezer is available for guests' use. (907) 747-8611; or fax (907) 747-5810. **$$**

■ **Super 8 Motel, 404 Sawmill Creek Road**

This independently operated national franchise offers comfortable, clean accommodations. Its 35 rooms include several suites. A free "toast bar" with breakfast foods is set out each morning in the lobby, and tea and coffee are available all day. Guests have use of a Jacuzzi spa and a coin-operated laundry. The second level of this motel is accessed by stairs, instead of elevator. Pets are allowed with a $50 refundable damage deposit. Guests paying by cash must make a $10 phone deposit at check-in for long-distance calls, the balance refunded at check-out. (907) 747-8804 (phone and fax). **$$**

■ Sitka Hotel, 118 Lincoln Street

This historic establishment, built in 1939, is one of the few older hotels left in Alaska. The hotel got a much-needed facelift with recent renovations, including recasting the lobby and foyer in Victorian-era decor, and new paint, carpet and windows throughout. Its 60 rooms

Sunlight filters through trees at Sitka National Historical Park. (Ernest Manewal)

include some with private baths; those with shared baths cost less. Some units have kitchenettes. Pets are sometimes allowed; inquire first. Sitka Hotel is located downtown, within walking distance of historic sites. **$**

OTHER LODGINGS

■ **Annahootz Bed and Breakfast, 111 Jeff Davis, P.O. Box 2870**
Located near Sheldon Jackson Museum and central to Sitka's other attractions, this bed-and-breakfast home offers two suites, each with private entrances, baths, sitting rooms and kitchenettes. The refrigerators are stocked daily with fruits, yogurts, homemade pastries, cereals and beverages for self-serve breakfasts. The home is owned by Dale Hanson, a well-established Alaska sculptor who works in his studio on the first floor. (907) 747-6498, (907) 747-8898 fax. **$$**

■ **Biorka Bed and Breakfast, 611 Biorka Street**
This modern home, located within three blocks of downtown attractions, has two quiet rooms, each with private baths and entries, phone and TV. Full breakfasts are served each morning to guests in their rooms. (907) 747-3111. **$$**

■ **Crescent Harbor Hideaway, 709 Lincoln Street**
This historic downtown home, overlooking Crescent Harbor, offers a furnished apartment and an upstairs guest room decorated with antiques—both with private entrances. Guests may relax in the home's glass-fronted porch facing the harbor; coffee, tea and snacks are always available, although no meals are served.
Originally owned by a gold miner, the home was Sitka's first with running water and indoor plumbing, which amounted to a pipe emptying onto the beach; a sign out front notes this history. Hosts Susan Stanford and Walt Cunningham, former commercial fishermen and marine mammal researchers, offer wildlife boat charters for an extra charge. (907) 747-4900. **$$**

■ **Alaska Ocean View Bed and Breakfast, 1101 Edgecumbe Drive**
This three-story lodging accommodates families with young children as well as couples looking for quiet romance.
The top floor Alaska Dogwood suite with king-size bed and private whirlpool tub faces the ocean and Mount

Edgecumbe. The smaller Sitka Rose Room, also on the top floor, is decorated in brass and wicker and faces the mountains. A winding staircase leads to the second level, where full breakfast buffets are served; guests may eat in the dining room, breakfast nook or on outside decks. The large Fireweed Room on this level has its own patio entrance and an adjacent play area equipped with children's toys, puzzles, videos, books and games.

An outdoor spa with Jacuzzi tub is available; terrycloth guest robes and slippers are provided. Along with ocean vistas, this hillside home offers good eagle viewing; for some reason eagles congregate by the dozens in this area of town, March through July. (907) 747-8310, phone and fax. **$$**

■ Creeks Edge Bed and Breakfast, 109 Cascade Creek Road

Country decor, antiques, feather beds and down comforters come with a view of Sitka Sound and Mount Edgecumbe at this bed and breakfast about 1.5 miles from downtown. An ocean-facing suite has a private deck and bath; one guest room has a private half-bath,

Rockwell Lighthouse provides a quiet island getaway just a short distance from town. (Ernest Manewal)

and two other rooms share a bath. All rooms have cable TV and phones. Guests are served full breakfasts. (907) 747-6484. **$$**

■ **Wild Strawberry Inn, 724 Siginaka Way, P.O. Box 2300**
This bed and breakfast inn/fishing lodge, located on Thomsen Harbor with a view of Mount Edgecumbe, is about a 10-minute walk from downtown. The inn's six upstairs rooms offer a variety of bed set-ups to accommodate groups of four or more per room; guests share three baths. Full, hot breakfasts are served each morning; guests may use the kitchen other times. A courtesy van runs between the inn, airport and ferry terminal. Guests paying with cash get a 4 percent discount. The inn also operates fishing and sightseeing boat charters for an additional charge. (907) 747-8883; or (907) 747-3646 fax. **$$**

■ **Youth Hostel, 303 Kimshan Street**
This economy lodging offers what amounts to indoor camping; bed linens are not provided, so bring a sleeping bag. The hostel, a member of the international group, operates June 1 through Aug. 30; doors open at 6 p.m. and guests must leave by 9:30 a.m. Smoking is not allowed; guests use a shared bath. (907) 747-8356. **$**

■ **Rockwell Lighthouse, P.O. Box 277**
This popular lighthouse lodging, built by a Sitka veterinarian as an island getaway, stays booked for summer visits at least a year in advance; winter reservations are easier to get on short notice.
The four-story structure with interior spiral staircase can comfortably sleep eight people, booked one party at a time. It has a whimsical nautical decor, down to a ship's wheel supporting the glass-topped kitchen table. The lighthouse has electricity—its red beacon is an operational navigation aid licensed by the U.S. Coast Guard—and a fully equipped kitchen, although guests need to bring their own food. Linens are provided, as are telephone, stereo with CD player and outdoor grill.
The view from the main front room looks past the island's rocky shore toward Mount Edgecumbe. The owner shuttles guests by boat to and from the island, or provides a skiff for their use. Along with great views of the ocean and a private

Campgrounds

Sawmill Creek Campground: Southeast of town off Sawmill Creek Road. At Sitka Pulp Mill, turn left on Blue Lake Road. The road is unmaintained, and not recommended for RVs. No fee; 14-day limit. Managed by U.S. Forest Service, Sitka Ranger District. Phone (907) 747-6671.

Sealing Cove RV Park: At Sealing Cove Harbor on Japonski Island near downtown Sitka. Maintained. $16/night plus tax. 26 sites with electric hookups. No reservations. Managed by City of Sitka. Phone (907) 747-3439.

Sitka Sportsman's Association RV Park: 200 feet south of ferry terminal on Halibut Point Road. Maintained. Pay. Phone (907) 747-6033.

Starrigavan Campground: 0.7 miles north of ferry dock. Maintained. Tent and RVs. $8/night; 14-day limit. U.S. Forest Service, Sitka Ranger District. Phone for information (907) 747-6671; for reservations (800) 280-CAMP.

Senior citizens are eligible for reduced rates at U.S. Forest Service campgrounds by presenting their Golden Age or Golden Eagle passports, available from Forest Service offices.

island to explore, guests can use the outside hot tub for a small extra charge. (907) 747-3056. **$$$**

■ Camp Coogan Bay Hideaway

A floating house provides a rustic sleepover in a secluded bay about six miles, or 20 minutes by skiff, from town. The cabin, on a 72-foot floating barge, sleeps eight on bunk beds and cots, with floor space available for more; there's a discount on rates if you provide sleeping bags instead of using the linens. An electric generator is available, but it makes a lot of noise in an otherwise quiet setting. The kitchen is equipped with a propane cooking stove, but no refrigerator; guests need to bring food. An outhouse serves as the bathroom. The float-house can be rented by the day or week, with or without a skiff for transportation to and from Sitka. Guests choosing to be dropped off will be given a radio to call for pickup. (907) 747-6375. **$$$** ■

So You're Hungry...

Here's an informal survey of some of Sitka's most popular restaurants, for both fine dining and casual noshing.

■ **Channel Club, 2906 Halibut Point Road**
Long known for its steaks and extensive salad bar, the Channel Club dates back to the days when loggers and fishermen came to town with big appetites for red meat. Other places in town serve steaks too, but none with the reputation of the Channel Club. It serves seafood and grilled chicken, as well. The big, open dining area joins the bar, and smoking is allowed. It's sometimes noisy with spotty service on busy nights, but its legend lives on. Open for dinner only. (907) 747-9916. **$$-$$$**

■ **The Marina Restaurant, 205 Harbor Drive**
The clam chowder served on Friday nights gets a nod

GUIDE TO PRICES

$ Inexpensive — less than $5
$$ Moderate — $6 to $15
$$$ Spendy — $16 to $40

In general, you should expect to pay these prices most anywhere in town:

Appetizers, $7 to $8	Coffee/Espresso drinks, $1 to $4
Sandwiches, $3 to $8	Desserts, with dinner, $2 to $4
Beer, $3 to $5	House wine, glass $3 to $4

from locals as the best in town, but that's not all that's cooking here under the watchful eye of owner Mike Lagos. The Marina does a fine job with seafood – shrimp sauté, white king salmon and halibut poached with artichoke hearts and capers in a wine sauce, for starters – as well as Italian dishes from pastas to pizzas. This upscale family restaurant has gorgeous decor with big bay windows overlooking Sitka Sound. A specially designed chair lift provides handicap access to the second floor entrance. Its large seating capacity for 120 is divided into small dining alcoves for smokers and non-smokers. It has a full bar and serves espresso. Open for lunch and dinner. (907) 747-8840. **$$-$$$**

■ Van Winkle and Daigler, 228 Harbor Drive

Another restaurant is making a reputation in Sitka with "frontier cuisine," yummy homemade desserts and gracious service. In addition to a regular menu, daily specials feature entrees such as Alaska bouillabaisse of king crab, oysters, clams, salmon and halibut, and lamb chops with feta cheese and spinach wrapped in puff pastry. Formerly Staton's Steak House, the kitchen has become more adventuresome under ownership of cousins Mike Daigler and Kirk Van Winkle, local boys who cooked their way around town and sea until buying this place in 1993. It's open for lunch and dinner, has a full service bar, and offers a quiet atmosphere where you can talk. (907) 747-3396. **$$-$$$**

■ Westmark Shee Atika Restaurant, 330 Seward Street

The restaurant serves what you'd expect from the best hotel in town: good food though rarely memorable, courteous service, tasteful surroundings. Like others in town, this restaurant taps the local market for fresh seafood. It opens early for breakfast, and lunch and dinner can be served in the bar as well as the dining room. The bar also has an hors d'oeuvres menu, plus select microbrews on tap. Diners can get a punch card for a free seventh meal, one reason the place does a good lunch trade with business people. (907) 747-6241. **$$-$$$**

■ Bayview Restaurant, 407 Lincoln Street

Located inside MacDonald's Bayview Trading Co., this eatery is a popular tourist lunch stop with tables on a balcony overlooking Crescent Harbor. A single-page double-sided menu offers fresh seafood, Russian-style foods, deli sandwiches, quiche, and hamburger and chicken sandwiches in almost every variation imaginable. The Bayview has an espresso bar and serves wine and beer, including imports and select domestic microbrews. Full-course breakfasts feature homemade Alaska pork sausage. (907) 747-5440. **$$**

■ El Dorado, 714 Katlian Street

Mexican food and homemade pizzas draw diners here, for eating in, take out or delivery. It's a steady favorite with all ages and occupations, maybe because of its extensive menu, more than 100 items from enchiladas to calzone to hamburgers, and don't forget the homemade pizzas in four sizes. The place seats 50 and is open seven days a week starting at 10:30 a.m., except major holidays. (907) 747-5070. **$$**

■ Twin Dragon Restaurant, 210 Katlian Street

If you're hungering for Chinese food, here's your best – and only – bet. It's open for lunch and dinner. (907) 747-5711. **$$-$$$**

■ Lulu's Diner, 116 Lincoln Street

This small refurbished '50s-style diner adjacent to the historic Sitka Hotel is a favorite breakfast spot for old-timers. Its menu is full of the expected diner standards; top sellers include a big biscuit topped with country gravy, and grilled chicken sandwiches accented with a variety of toppings. Open through dinner with daily specials, Lulu's also serves beer and wine. (907) 747-5628. **$-$$**

■ Lane 7, 331 Lincoln Street

This tiny grill inside the bowling alley may have the best milkshakes in town, certainly the most flavors with 25 on the menu. They're made with old-fashioned, hard ice cream and served with fruit toppings. The family-owned operation seats 21 people at four tables and a counter, and does a big carry-out business. The menu includes hamburgers, vegetarian garden burgers, grilled chicken sandwiches, halibut-and-chips, and a passel of deep-fried side orders from fries to zucchini. Lane 7 is a secret favorite of many Sitkans. (907) 747-6310. **$-$$**

■ **Ginny's Kitchen, 236 Lincoln Street**

Owner Ginny Wood has been serving customers here, across from St. Michael's Cathedral, for about 25 years. Homemade soups and deli sandwiches made with breads and rolls baked fresh on premises are the big sellers. The place offers continental breakfasts and stays open for dinner in summer, with hot specials daily. You can also get espresso drinks, along with a variety of confections including milkshakes—made with real ice cream on request. (907) 747-8028. **$-$$**

■ **Coffee Express, 104 Lake Street**

This cozy espresso shop, also owned by Ginny Wood, offers soups, sandwiches, sweet treats and all sorts of specialty tea and coffee drinks in a smoke-free environment, across from the Westmark Shee Atika Hotel. (907) 747-3343. **$-$$**

■ **The Back Door, 104 Barracks**

This espresso, sandwich and pastry shop is favored by Sitka's alternative crowd, the eco-hippy types who talk local politics and trade kayaking stories, as well as commercial fishermen and downtown shop owners. Specials change weekly, including fresh bagel sandwiches, with soups in winter. Mouthwatering baked goods—salmonberry scones; fruit pound cakes; date bars; big chocolate chip cookies; Kona muffins made with espresso, coconut and walnuts— come from ovens here and at **The Mojo Cafe**, 256 Katlian Street, a bakery with a small lunch counter, under the same ownership. Both places are smoke-free. Inconspicuously located behind Old Harbor Books with few signs to point the way, The Back Door is open daily, 7 a.m. to 5 p.m., except Sundays when it opens later and closes at 1 p.m. On some Thursdays, it reopens at 7 p.m. when local musicians take the stage. (907) 747-8856. **$**

■ **The Kingfisher Cafe, 201 Katlian Street (Totem Square)**

One of the newest coffeehouses to join the espresso scene downtown features grilled sandwiches made with Italian foccacia bread, cold halibut salad and deli meat lunchables. Specialty coffees, teas and juices and fresh bakery items round out the menu. Its non-smoking environment includes two tables outside on nice days with a view of the Pioneer Home and Russian blockhouse. (907) 747-4888. **$-$$**

■ **The Nugget Restaurant, Airport Terminal**

This restaurant serves mainly the airport crowd, and through the years has made a name with its fresh-baked pies. About 45 pies a day go out the door, in slices or whole, most with travelers. Peanut butter, fresh strawberry, strawberry-rhubarb, and banana cream are the unofficial top sellers. The restaurant serves breakfast and dinner. (907) 966-2480. **$-$$**

■ **McDonald's, 913 Halibut Point Road**

You get what you expect under the famous golden arches, plus a twist in environment and menu. Located right on Sitka Sound, it may have the best view of any McDonald's in the nation. It also offers five varieties of pizza (some fans say the best in town), soup and chili, and fried chicken. Hamburgers are only 50 cents on Friday and Saturday nights. This is one of two national franchise restaurants to make it to Sitka. (907) 747-8709. **$-$$**

■ **Subway Sandwiches, 327 Seward**

Here's the second. It's made its reputation with its built-to-order deli sandwiches, complete with its own version of kid's meals. (907) 747-7827. **$-$$**

■ **Rookies Sports Bar & Grill, 1617 Sawmill Creek Road**

Formerly the raucous rock 'n' roll Kiksadi Club, this roadhouse 2.5 miles out of town recently underwent a change of ownership and attitude. It's now Rookies with a 65-item menu covering all the bases – sandwiches, pasta, seafood and salad – and a sports motif, seven TVs hanging from above and a big screen always tuned to sports. Rookies also has sports games, like darts, air hockey, pool, foos ball. The burgers rate high with some in town, and the bar offers a selection of microbrews. It's open for lunch and dinner with the kitchen cooking until 1 a.m. A disc jockey lays tracks for the party crowd late at night, with live bands taking the stage several times a year. Comedy nights, once a week through winter, feature imported jokesters. (907) 747-7607. **$$-$$$**

■ **Sea Mart Super, 1867 Halibut Point Road**

A newly remodeled deli at the largest grocery in Sitka features a dining area with tables overlooking the water and Mount Edgecumbe, as well as take-out service. The deli serves an assortment of sandwich meats, salads, cheeses and bakery goods, as well as oriental food, pizza, fried chicken and soft-serve yogurt. Party trays are available, and drinks include fountain sodas, juices and espresso. Deli hours are 7 a.m. to 7 p.m., although the grocery stays open until 9 p.m., seven days a week. (907) 747-6266 **$-$$**

■ Sea Mart Downtown, 210 Baranof

The deli in this downtown grocery has sandwiches, bagels, an assortment of salads, baked goods, and reheatable entrees for take-out only. It's open 5 a.m. to midnight in summer; 6 a.m. to 11 p.m. in winter. (907) 747-6686. **$-$$**

■ Lakeside Grocery, 705 Halibut Point Road

A small deli/bakery in this grocery serves hot lunches, sandwiches, soups and has a salad bar. It's mostly aimed at take-out orders, although there are several tables for eating in. Deli hours are 6 a.m. to 9 p.m.; the grocery stays open until midnight. (907) 747-3317. **$-$$**

■ Cascade Convenience Center, 2035 Halibut Point Road

The grill at this small grocery fires up at 4 p.m. for burgers, fresh-made pizza, tacos and stir-fry, for take-out orders only. Sandwiches are available earlier in the day. The grill goes until midnight. The store is open 6 a.m. to 2 a.m. (907) 747 8313. **$-$$** ■

Sitka beaches are carpeted with small shells. (Dan Evans)

For More Information

■ VISITOR SERVICES

Sitka assesses a 4 percent sales tax and a 4 percent bed tax.

Sitka Convention and Visitors Bureau:
P.O. Box 1226, Sitka 99835. Phone (907) 747-5940; fax. (907) 747-3739. They operate a visitor information booth at the Centennial Building, phone (907) 747-3225. Call Centennial Building phone number to arrange baggage storage for a minimum fee.

Sitka Chamber of Commerce:
Centennial Building, 330 Harbor Dr., Sitka 99835. Phone (907) 747-8604.

Alaska Division of Parks and Outdoor Recreation:
P.O. Box 142, Sitka 99835. Phone (907) 747 6249.

National Park Service:
Sitka National Historical Park, 106 Metlakatla, P.O. Box 738, Sitka 99835. Phone (907) 747-6281.

U.S. Forest Service:
Sitka Ranger District, Tongass National Forest, 201 Katlian, Suite 109, Sitka 99835. Phone (907) 747-6671.
Hoonah Ranger District, Tongass National Forest, P.O. Box 135, Hoonah 99829. Phone (907) 945-3631.
Forest Supervisor—Chatham Area, Tongass National Forest: 204 Siginaka Way, Sitka 99835. Phone (907) 747-6671.

Alaska Department of Fish and Game, Sport Fish Division:
304 Lake St., Room 103, Sitka 99835. Phone (907) 747-5355.

National Weather Service:
(907) 747-6011 (recording of local and marine forecasts).

Sitka Harbormaster:
617 Katlian Street, Sitka 99835. Phone (907) 747-3439.

■ POLICE/MEDICAL/EMERGENCY

Dial 911 in emergencies to contact police, fire department and ambulances. The U.S. Coast Guard Air Station and the Sitka Harbormaster also monitor Channel 16 on VHF radio for marine emergencies.

Alaska State Troopers, 877 Sawmill Creek Road, Sitka 99835. Phone (907) 747-6611.

Sitka Police Department, 304 Lake Street, Sitka 99835. Phone (907) 747-3245.

Sitka Fire Department, 209 Lake Street, Sitka 99835. Phone (907) 747-3233.

U.S. Coast Guard Air Station, 611 Airport Road, Sitka 99835. Phone (907) 966-5420 for information. Phone (907) 966-5555 for emergencies.

Sitka Community Hospital, 209 Moller Drive, Sitka 99835. Phone (907) 747-3241.

Mount Edgecumbe Hospital/Southeast Alaska Regional Health Corp., 222 Tongass Drive, Sitka 99835. Phone (907) 966-2411.

■ BANKS/ATMS:

First Bank, 208C Lake Street, Sitka 99835. ATM accessible all hours. Phone (907) 747-6636; fax (907) 747-6635.

First National Bank, 318 Lincoln Street, Sitka 99835. ATM accessible all hours. Phone (907) 747-3272; fax (907) 747-1449.

Post Offices

Main Branch: 1207 Sawmill Creek Road. Hours 9 a.m. to 5 p.m.

Substation: Macdonald's Bayview Trading Co., 407 Lincoln. Hours 9 a.m. to 6 p.m.

Substation: Totem Square Bldg., Totem Square Complex, 201 Katlian. Hours 9 a.m. to 5 p.m.

National Bank of Alaska, 300 Lincoln Street, Sitka 99835. ATM accessible all hours. Phone (907) 747-3226; fax (907) 747-8081.

Alaska Federal Savings and Loan Association, 101 Lake Street, Sitka 99835. Phone (907) 747-8688.

A park service employee talks to Alaska Day visitors to the Russian Bishop's House. (Ernest Manewal)

■ MEDIA

Newspapers:
Daily Sitka Sentinel, 112 Barracks Street, Sitka 99835. Phone (907) 747-3219; fax (907) 747-8898. Published Monday through Friday; 50 cents a copy.

Radio:
KCAW (90.1 and 104.7 FM), 2B Lincoln Street, Sitka 99835. National Public Radio affiliate. Phone (907) 747-5877.

KIFW (1230 AM)/KSBZ (103.1 FM), 611 Lake Street, Sitka 99835. Phone (907) 747-6626.

Broadcast Television:
KTNL Channel 13, P.O. Box 1309, Sitka 99835. The local CBS affiliate. Phone (907) 747-6002.

KSCT Channel 5, 520 Lake Street, Sitka 99835. The local FOX affiliate and Sitka Community Television. Phone (907) 747-8200.

Cable Television:
Alaskan Cable Network, 208A Lake Street, Sitka 99835, provides cable TV access, with 45 channels including the two local broadcast channels, EPSN, HBO, etc. Phone (907) 747-3535.

■ CHURCHES

Sitka has more than 20 churches representing all the major denominations including **Roman Catholic, Episcopal, Methodist, Lutheran, Presbyterian, Baptist, Church of Jesus Christ of Latter-Day Saints, Russian Orthodox** and **Baha'i.**

■ GETTING TO SITKA

Alaska Marine Highway, P.O. Box 25535, Juneau 99802-5535. Phone (800) 642-0066; in Sitka (907) 747-8737.

Alaska Airlines, Phone (800) 426-0333; in Sitka (907) 966-2266.

A yacht cruises into Sitka Channel. (Ernest Manewal)

■ GETTING AROUND SITKA

Car Rentals:
Prices range from $35 to $50 a day with unlimited mileage.
Advantage Car Rentals, Airport Terminal, Sitka 99835.
Phone (907) 747-7557.
Allstar Rent-A-Car, 600-C Airport Road, Sitka 99835.
Phone (907) 966-2552.
Avis Rent-A-Car, Airport Desk, Mt. Edgecumbe 99835.
Phone (907) 966-2404; (800) 331-1212.
Baranof Motors, 1209 Sawmill Creek Road, Sitka 99835.
Phone (907) 747-8228.

Ground Taxis:
Base rates inside Sitka city limits start at $3.50 with an
additional 50 cents to 75 cents for each additional passenger.
The fare from the airport to downtown is $6; a ride from the
ferry to downtown costs $13. Fares to outlying destinations
on the road system vary. Charter rates range from $20 for a
half day, to $40 for a full day.
Arrowhead Taxi, P.O. Box 1497, Sitka 99835. Phone (907)
747-8888.
Sitka Cabs Inc., 128 Lincoln, Sitka 99835. Phone (907)
747-5001.

Shuttle Buses:
Rates range from $2.50 one-way to $5 round-trip. The
airport shuttle meets all flights May through October; the
ferry transit meets each ferry year-round.
Ferry Transit Bus & Airport Shuttle Bus, Sitka Tours, Box
1001, Sitka 99835. Phone (907) 747-8443.

Air Transportation:
Two air taxi companies operate from Sitka to serve
outlying destinations, including smaller Southeast villages
and towns, Forest Service cabins and remote camps. Rates
start at $65 one-way for regularly scheduled flights to towns,
and range between $250 and $580 an hour for airplane or
helicopter charters.
Bellair Inc., Box 371 or 485 Katlian, Sitka 99835. Phone
(907) 747-8636 or 747-3220; fax (907) 747-6090.
Mountain Aviation Inc., Box 2487, Sitka 99835. Phone (907)
966-2288 or (800) 210-2288 (in Alaska); fax (907) 966-2299. ■

Bibliography

See the following quarterly issues of *ALASKA GEOGRAPHIC®* for more information on Sitka, its environment, wildlife and Native cultures. (See page 140 for information on ordering available back issues of *ALASKA GEOGRAPHIC®*.)

Alaska Whales and Whaling. 1978.
Alaska's Native Arts and Crafts. 1985.
Alaska's Native People. 1979.
Alaska's Volcanoes. 1991.
Sitka and its Ocean / Island World. 1982.
Southeast Alaska. 1993.

Other Selections

Andrews, C.L. Sitka, *The Chief Factory of the Russian American Company.* Third edition. Caldwell, Idaho: Caxton Printers, Ltd., 1945.

—. *The Story of Sitka.* Seattle: Loman & Hanford Co., 1922.

DeArmond, R.N., editor. *Early Visitors to Southeastern Alaska.* Anchorage: Alaska Northwest Publishing Co., 1978.

—. *From Sitka's Past.* Sitka, Alaska: Sitka Historical Society, 1995.

—. *Lady Franklin Visits Sitka, Alaska 1870, the Journal of Sophia Cracroft, Sir John Franklin's Niece.* Anchorage: Alaska Historical Society, 1981.

Emmons, George T. *The Tlingit Indians*. Frederica deLaguna, ed., Seattle, New York: University of Washington Press and American Museum of Natural History, 1991.

Fedorova, Svetlana. *Russian Population in Alaska and California: Late 18th Century-1867*. Richard A. Pierce and Alton S. Donnelly, translators. Kingston, Ontario: Limestone Press, 1973.

Golovin, Pavel N. *Civil and Savage Encounters: The Worldly Travel Letters of an Imperial Russian Navy Officer, 1860-1861*. Basil Dmytryshyn and E.A.P. Crownhart-Vaughan, translators and editors. Portland: Oregon Historical Society, 1983.

Hoagland, Alison K. *Buildings of Alaska*. New York: Oxford University Press, 1993.

Holm, Bill. *Northwest Coast Indian Art*. Seattle: University of Washington Press, 1965.

Khlebnikov, K.T. *Colonial Russian America, Kyrill T. Khlebnikov's Reports, 1817-1832*. Basil Dmytryshyn and E.A.P. Crownhart-Vaughan, translators. Portland: Oregon Historical Society, 1976.

Olson, Wallace M. *The Tlingit: An introduction to their culture and history*. Juneau: Heritage Research, 1993.

Piggott, Margaret. *Discover Southeast with Pack & Paddle*. Seattle: The Mountaineers, 1990.

Scidmore, Eliza Ruhamah. *Alaska and Its Southern Coast*. Boston: D. Lotherop and Co., 1885.

Smith, Barabara Sweetland and Redmond J. Barnett. *Russian America: The Forgotten Frontier*. Tacoma, Wash.: Washington State Historical Society, 1990.

Stewart, Hilary. *Looking at Totem Poles*. Seattle: University of Washington Press, 1993.

Willoughby, Barrett. *Sitka—Portal to Romance*. Boston and New York: Houghton Mifflin Co., 1930. ■

The **ALASKA GEOGRAPHIC** Library

The Alaska Geographic Society is a non-profit, educational organization dedicated to improving geographic understanding of Alaska and the North. Each year The Society publishes four *ALASKA GEOGRAPHIC®* books full of information and colorful photographs, each book focusing on a particular geographic region or resource-related topic. The Society has published nearly 90 high-quality books since its founding in 1968; of these, the nearly 60 titles listed below are available today.

Society members receive a subscription to the *ALASKA GEOGRAPHIC®* quarterly as part of their $39 annual membership. In addition, these award-winning, informative books are sold in bookstores and specialty shops worldwide.

Other benefits for Alaska Geographic Society members include a valuable 20 percent members discount, which can be applied to purchases of *ALASKA GEOGRAPHIC®* back issues and other books published by The Society, as well as an assortment of carefully selected, top quality merchandise, such as videos, maps and gift items, available through The Society. To learn more about these other items, write or call for our complete catalog. To order any of the books listed below, see instructions on page 140.

■ ■ ■

Admiralty: Island in Contention, Vol. 1, No. 3. A review of Southeast's Admiralty Island: its geology and historical past, its present-day geography, wildlife and sparse human population. 78 pages, $7.95.

Richard Harrington's Antarctic, Vol. 3, No. 3. Canadian photojournalist Harrington takes readers through the remote regions of the Antarctic and Subantarctic. More than 200 color photos. 104 pages, $17.95.

The Silver Years of the Alaska Canned Salmon Industry: An Album of Historical Photos, Vol. 3, No. 4. This issue commemorates the heyday of the salmon canning industry from the late 1800s to 1970s with text and more than 450 historic photos. 168 pages, $17.95.

Alaska Whales and Whaling, Vol. 5, No. 4. An examination of whales in Alaska, their life cycles, travels and travails, and whaling in the North. Includes a fold-out poster of 14 whale species in Alaska. 144 pages, $19.95.

Aurora Borealis: The Amazing Northern Lights, Vol. 6, No. 2. Dr. S. I. Akasofu of the University of Alaska, Fairbanks, a leading expert on the aurora, explains in simple terms what causes the aurora, how it works and how and why scientists are studying it. With index; 96 pages, $19.95.

Alaska's Native People, Vol. 6, No. 3. Examines the worlds of the Inupiat Eskimo, Yup'ik Eskimo, Athabascan, Aleut, Haida, Tlingit and Tsimshian. Includes a large, color map. 304 pages, $24.95. **LIMITED SUPPLY.**

The Stikine River, Vol. 6, No. 4. Route to 1800s gold strikes, the Stikine is the largest and most navigable river flowing from Canada through Southeastern Alaska and to the Pacific. With fold-out map; 96 pages, $17.95.

Alaska's Great Interior, Vol. 7, No. 1. An overview of the region between the Alaska and Brooks ranges, including Fairbanks, its economic hub; area rivers; communities and history. With fold-out map; 128 pages, $17.95.

Alaska National Interest Lands, Vol. 8, No. 4. Reviews each of Alaska's national interest land selections (d-2 lands), outlining their location, size and access and briefly describing special attractions. 242 pages, $17.95.

Alaska's Glaciers, Vol. 9, No. 1. (Revised 1993) Examines glaciers in-depth, their composition, exploration, distribution and scientific significance. With diagrams, color and historical photos. With index; 144 pages, $19.95.

Islands of the Seals: The Pribilofs, Vol. 9, No. 3. Herds of northern fur seals and flocks of seabirds drew Russians to these remote islands where they founded permanent communities. 128 pages, $17.95.

Alaska's Oil/Gas & Minerals Industry, Vol. 9. No. 4. Experts detail the geological processes and resulting mineral and fossil fuel resources that contribute substantially to Alaska's economy. 216 pages, $17.95.

Adventure Roads North: The Story of the Alaska Highway and Other Roads in The Milepost, Vol. 10, No. 1. From Alaska's first highway, the Richardson, to the famous Alaska Highway (Alcan), this issue reviews Alaska's roads and the country they cross. 224 pages, $17.95.

Anchorage and the Cook Inlet Basin, Vol. 10, No. 2. An in-depth review of this commercial and urban center of Alaska. Heavily illustrated with color photos; comes with two fold-out posters and one map. 168 pages, $17.95.

Alaska's Salmon Fisheries, Vol. 10. No. 3. A comprehensive look at Alaska's most valuable commercial fishery, including a district-by-district tour of salmon fisheries throughout the state. 128 pages, $17.95.

Up the Koyukuk, Vol. 10, No. 4. A thorough exploration of the vast drainage of the Koyukuk River, third largest in Alaska. 152 pages, $17.95.

Nome: City of the Golden Beaches, Vol. 11, No. 1. Reviews the colorful history of one of Alaska's most famous gold rush towns. Includes nearly 200 historical black-and-white photos. 184 pages, $17.95.

Alaska's Farms and Gardens, Vol. 11, No. 2. An overview of the past, present and future of agriculture in Alaska, with a wealth of information on growing fruits and vegetables in the Far North. 144 pages, $17.95.

Chilkat River Valley, Vol. 11, No. 3. Explores the mountain-rimmed valley at the head of the Inside Passage, including the huge numbers of bald eagles that congregate there each year. 112 pages, $17.95.

Alaska Steam, Vol. 11, No. 4. The inspiring history of the Alaska Steamship Co. and the pioneers who navigated the hazardous waters of the northern travel lanes to serve the people of Alaska. 160 pages, $17.95.

Northwest Territories, Vol. 12, No. 1. A detailed look at Canada's immense Northwest Territories, site of some of the most beautiful and isolated land in North America. With fold-out map; 136 pages, $17.95.

Alaska's Forest Resources, Vol. 12, No. 2. A close look at the economic, botanical, and recreational value of Alaska's forests. Includes a section on identification of the state's 33 native tree species. 200 pages, $17.95.

Alaska Native Arts and Crafts, Vol. 12, No. 3. Offers an in-depth review of the art and artifacts of Alaska's Native people. Artwork is illustrated in more than 200 color photos. 216 pages, $22.95. **LIMITED SUPPLY.**

Our Arctic Year, Vol. 12, No. 4. Vivian and Gil Staender's simple, compelling story of their year in the wilds of Alaska's Brooks Range, with only birds, nature and an unspoiled landscape. 150 pages, $17.95.

Where Mountains Meet the Sea: Alaska's Gulf Coast, Vol. 13, No. 1. First-hand descriptions of the 850-mile arc of coastline stretching from Kodiak to Cape Spencer at the entrance to the Inside Passage. 192 pages, $17.95.

Backcountry Alaska, Vol. 13, No. 2. A full-color look at Alaska's remote communities, including how to get there, what to do and where to stay. 224 pages, $17.95.

British Columbia's Coast, Vol. 13, No. 3. A look at Canada's gold coast and the Canadian portion of the Inside Passage, including the Queen Charlotte Islands. With fold-out map; 200 pages, $17.95.

Dogs of the North, Vol. 14, No. 1. Examines the development of northern dog breeds and evolution of sled-dog racing, including the internationally known Iditarod Trail Sled Dog Race. 120 pages, $17.95. **LIMITED SUPPLY.**

Alaska's Seward Peninsula, Vol. 14, No. 3. This issue chronicles the blending of the Eskimo culture with the white man's search for gold. With fold-out map; 112 pages, $17.95.

The Upper Yukon Basin, Vol. 14, No. 4. A description of the remote area surrounding the headwaters of one of the continent's mightiest rivers and gateway for Alaska's early pioneers. 120 pages, $17.95. **LIMITED SUPPLY.**

Dawson City, Vol. 15, No. 2. Author Mike Doogan relates the colorful history of the Klondike gold rush and takes a look at Dawson City today. Historical and contemporary photos. With index; 96 pages, $17.95.

Denali, Vol. 15, No. 3. Provides an in-depth look at the 20,320-foot crown of the Alaska Range, its lofty nieghbors and surrounding parklands and wilderness areas. With fold-out map and index; 96 pages, $19.95.

The Kuskokwim River, Vol. 15, No. 4. Reviews one of Alaska's most important rivers, from its headwaters in the Kuskokwim Mountains to its mouth on Kuskokwim Bay. With fold-out map and index; 96 pages, $17.95.

Katmai Country, Vol. 16, No. 1. This issue examines the volcanic world of Katmai National Park and Preserve and adjoining Becharof National Wildlife Refuge.With fold-out map and index; 96 pages, $17.95.

North Slope Now, Vol. 16, No. 2. This issue brings readers up to date on the economic and political forces that have shaped the North Slope. With fold-out map and index; 96 pages, $17.95.

The Tanana Basin, Vol. 16, No. 3. A review of this urban center of interior Alaska. Includes reviews of the lifestyle and history of this portion of Alaska's heartland. With fold-out map and index; 96 pages, $17.95.

The Copper Trail, Vol. 16, No. 4. This issue examines the Kennecott copper deposits, Copper River & Northwestern Railway, Cordova, southeastern Prince William Sound. With fold-out map and index; 96 pages, $17.95.

The Nushagak River, Vol. 17, No. 1. Reviews this important corridor, and details the lifestyle and resources of this site of one of the world's largest commercial fisheries. With fold-out map and index; 96 pages, $17.95.

The Middle Yukon River, Vol. 17, No. 3. Follows the course of the Yukon from Fortymile, near the Canadian border, down river to Holy Cross. With fold-out map and index; 96 pages, $17.95.

The Lower Yukon River, Vol. 17, No. 4. From Holy Cross, this issue traces the serpentine route of the Yukon through its braided delta to the mouth on the Bering Sea. With index; 96 pages, $17.95.

Alaska's Weather, Vol. 18, No. 1. Helps readers answer that often-asked question: "What's the weather like?" Also provides glimpses into the ways in which Alaskans cope with their climate. With index; 96 pages, $17.95.

Alaska's Volcanoes, Vol. 18, No. 2. This scientific overview of Alaska's portion of the Ring of Fire brings readers up to date on the activities of the state's dynamic volcanoes. With index; 96 pages, $17.95.

Admiralty Island...Fortress of the Bears, Vol. 18, No. 3. Examines this wilderness/wildlife sanctuary, site of significant mineral wealth and thick forests. With fold-out map and index; 96 pages, $17.95. **LIMITED SUPPLY.**

Unalaska/Dutch Harbor, Vol. 18, No. 4. Commercial heart of the Aleutian Islands, Unalaska and its Port of Dutch Harbor prosper as a gateway to the Aleutians and western Alaska. With index; 96 pages, $18.95.

Skagway: A Legacy of Gold, Vol. 19, No. 1. Jumping off point for the Klondike gold rush, Skagway has seen its fortunes rise, fall and rise again. With index; 96 pages, $18.95.

Alaska: The Great Land, Vol. 19, No. 2. This issue offers an overview of Alaska's six diverse regions, from the islands of Southeast, to the snow-swept Arctic, to the remote Aleutians. With index; 112 pages, $18.95.

Kodiak, Vol. 19, No. 3. One of Alaska's largest communities, fierce wildlife, rugged wilderness and wild waters make up the Kodiak archipelago. With index; 112 pages, $18.95. **LIMITED SUPPLY.**

Alaska's Railroads, Vol. 19, No. 4. This issue looks at the lines that contributed to Alaska's railroad history, and assesses their economic impact on the state. With index; 96 pages, $18.95.

Prince William Sound, Vol. 20, No. 1. This issue looks at the region's resources; its economic hub, Valdez; its people; and its spectacular scenery. With index; 112 pages, $18.95.

Southeast Alaska, Vol. 20, No. 2. Explores the waterways and mountain tops that make up Alaska's scenic Panhandle. Includes a profile of Juneau, Alaska's capital. With fold-out map and index; 128 pages, $19.95.

Arctic National Wildlife Refuge, Vol. 20, No. 3. This issue details the region's natural resources, human use of those resources and the politics that make this remote area so controversial. With index; 96 pages, $18.95.

Alaska's Bears, Vol. 20, No. 4. Details the natural history of Alaska's three species of bears—brown/grizzly, black and polar. With index; 112 pages, $18.95.

The Alaska Peninsula, Vol. 21, No. 1. Active and dormant volcanoes, hidden bays, abundant fish and wildlife and a handful of remote communities characterize the rugged Alaska Peninsula. With index; 96 pages, $19.95.

Kenai Peninsula, Vol. 21, No. 2. This peninsula embraces the traditional Alaska of hunters, fishermen and homesteaders, as well as the modern Alaska fueled by the oil and gas industries. With index; 128 pages, $19.95.

People of Alaska, Vol. 21, No. 3. A chronicle of Alaska's people, from early-day Natives to modern boomers who forge the state's future. With index; 96 pages, $19.95.

Prehistoric Alaska, Vol. 21, No. 4. An up-to-date account of Alaska's land formation, plus the dinosaurs, prehistoric mammals and people who survived here before recorded history. With index; 112 pages, $19.95.

Fairbanks, Vol. 22, No. 1. From its origin as a mining supply depot on the Chena River, Fairbanks has grown into the service and supply center for Alaska's Interior and North. With index; 96 pages, $19.95.

The Aleutian Islands, Vol. 22, No. 2. Details this remote region from the Russians who came more than 250 years ago to today's busy commercial fishing fleets. With fold-out map and index; 112 pages, $19.95.

Rich Earth: Alaska's Mineral Industry, Vol. 22, No. 3. Explores past and present mining in Alaska; from placer and hardrock mining for gold and other minerals to the mining of industrial minerals. With index; $19.95.

World War II in Alaska, Vol. 22, No. 4. An in-depth account of the war in Alaska, including construction of the Alaska Highway, the military buildup and the Japanese invasion of the Aleutians. With index; $19.95.

Anchorage, Vol. 23, No. 1. A comprehensive review of Alaska's largest city: its setting, commerce and transportation, along with its people, culture, recreation and tourism. With index; $19.95. [Available 4/96]

Native Cultures In Alaska, Vol. 23, No. 2. A look at the traditional lifestyles and rich heritage of Alaska's Native people, including their hopes for the future. With index; $19.95. [Available 7/96]

The Brooks Range, Vol. 23, No. 3. This issue offers a comprehensive look at the largest mountain range in northern Alaska. With index; $19.95. [Available 9/96]

Moose, Caribou and Musk Ox, Vol. 23, No. 4. An in-depth exploration of the natural history and life cycles of Alaska's largest ungulates along with traditional uses of the animals. With index; $19.95. [Available 12/96]

■ ■ ■

To become an Alaska Geographic Society member or to order any of the *ALASKA GEOGRAPHIC*® books listed above, send us your name and address, a list of books you'd like, and your payment (check or money order in U.S. funds or VISA or MasterCard number and expiration date). Add shipping and handling of $2 per book for book rate postage or $4 per book for Priority Mail. Send orders to:

ALASKA GEOGRAPHIC SOCIETY
P.O. Box 93370-SG, Anchorage AK 99509 • (907) 562-0164

Index

A setting sun highlights totems at Sitka National Historical Park. (Scott Chambers)

Three friends tote their catch from the shore of Starrigavan Bay. (Ernest Manewal)